A Vast Minority

A Vast Minority

Christians in Post-Christendom Britain

Stuart Murray

Paternoster:
thinking faith

21 20 19 18 17 16 15 7 6 5 4 3 2 1

First published 2015 by Paternoster
Paternoster is an imprint of Authentic Media Limited
52 Presley Way, Crownhill, Milton Keynes, MK8 0ES.
authenticmedia.co.uk

British Library Cataloguing in Publication Data

A catalogue record for this book is available from the British Library

ISBN 978-1-84227-837-6
978-1-78078-0-863 (e-book)

Cover Design by David McNeill (www.revocreative.co.uk)
Printed and bound by CPI Group (UK) Ltd., Croydon, CR0 4YY

Contents

Preface

I spent quite a while looking for resources on the subject of this book – but without much success. There is material from minority Christian communities in other parts of the world. There are insights from other minority communities in various times and places. But there is very little that addresses the issue the Christian community in Britain (and other Western societies) is facing: how to transition from a majority community to a minority community. I believe this is a critical issue with huge theological, missiological and ecclesial implications. It impacts the strategies, priorities, resources, expectations, morale and self-identity of the Christian community. It offers great opportunities but poses significant challenges. When I mentioned what I was exploring, people were intrigued and encouraged me to invest time and energy in this. When I asked if they knew of any relevant resources, I almost always drew a blank.

So I ended up writing the book I was searching for – pulling together what resources I could find, reflecting on biblical texts that seemed pertinent, talking with others who were aware of this issue, and drawing on my own experience. I am under no illusion that this is the last word on the subject or even a comprehensive exploration of the many questions we need to ask as we come to terms with this change in our status. But I hope it will highlight some of the main issues, spark debate and encourage further reflection. Some of what I have written is tentative and some may be regarded as controversial. Some is critical of current and emerging policies and practices; but I hope my tone is as measured and gracious as I have intended. I welcome dialogue and look forward to learning from others as we continue to explore what it means to be an ex-majority Christian community.

As in most of the books I have written, I draw gratefully (if not as explicitly as sometimes) on the Anabaptist tradition – a minority tradition many are rediscovering that has much to teach us, especially in the areas of ethics and ecclesiology. My own ecclesial roots are in the Open Brethren movement that emerged in the mid-nineteenth century, one of many movements in church history yearning for a simpler expression of church and greater coherence with New Testament ecclesiology. For the past twenty years I have been in membership of a number of Baptist churches. And for the past thirty-five years I have been committed to and involved in various ways in urban ministry, church planting and theological education. I am sure my nonconformist background and convictions will be evident in what follows. But I am convinced we will need the insights and resources of many traditions as we learn to live as a creative, prophetic and hopeful minority Christian community.

I am grateful also to those who kindly read the manuscript and offered various corrective and creative insights. These insights have improved the book. But, of course, I am responsible for the final text with the deficiencies that remain.

Stuart Murray
December 2014

Introduction

Estimates vary, but possibly 10 per cent of the population of the Roman Empire identified themselves as Christians in the year 315. If so, this meant roughly six million believers lived among the sixty million or so who made up this sprawling, multi-ethnic, multi-religious empire. There were stronger Christian communities in some parts of the empire than others. The east had a significantly higher proportion of Christians than the west, and many of the cities had had greater exposure to the gospel than most rural areas.

The Christian community was a minority in 315, but it was a vast minority – large enough to persuade the new emperor, Constantine I, to ally himself with it. Not only did he remove from it the threat of persecution – bringing to an end nearly three centuries of illegality, secrecy and uncertainty – but he also identified himself as a Christian, heaped favours and resources on the churches, and invited church leaders to help him unite his fragmented realm and breathe new life into a weary culture. In 315 his huge triumphal arch in Rome was completed, celebrating the victory over his rival, Maxentius, that secured for him the imperial throne.

Fast forward seventeen hundred years to 2015. Estimates again vary and there are disputes over definitions, but possibly 10 per cent of the population of Britain can plausibly be considered followers of Jesus. As in 315, this might equate to six million out of a little over sixty million who make up an increasingly multi-ethnic, multi-religious and also secular society. Christian communities are stronger in some areas than others, with suburban neighbourhoods and small towns having up to ten times as many Christian residents as some inner-city areas and housing estates.

After centuries of cultural dominance in Western societies and a near-monopoly on religious allegiance in the era historians call 'Christendom', the Christian community in what many now refer to as 'post-Christendom' is once again a minority – albeit a vast minority. It still comprises many millions across the region that once constituted Christendom, but it may be approximately the same size in Britain as it was in the 'pre-Christendom' Roman Empire.

The parallels are striking, but so are the differences:

- In 315, the Christian community had been experiencing rapid and sustained growth for many decades; in 2015, it has known slow but persistent decline over many years.
- In 315, the Christian community was stronger in the cities and much weaker in the countryside; in 2015, it is stronger in the suburbs while large areas of our cities and many rural areas are almost devoid of Christian witness.
- In 315, memories of persecution were still fresh and imperial endorsement was a new and unanticipated factor that some welcomed and others feared; in 2015, memories of social and cultural privilege are still fresh, and the loss of these privileges provokes grief, anger, resentment and murmurings (however ludicrous) about persecution.
- In 315, very few would claim to be Christians or participate in the activities of the Christian community unless they were serious about their faith; in 2015, the term has been so debased and domesticated that those who are serious about their faith often prefer to call themselves 'followers of Jesus'.
- In 315, most people subscribed to some form of religious belief and Christians were called 'atheists' because of their refusal to embrace the imperial ideology; in 2015, despite the prevalence of an inchoate spirituality that resists demarcation, growing numbers answer 'no religion' when asked about their beliefs, but most expressions of atheism offer no effective resistance to contemporary ideologies.
- In 315, the church had only ever been a minority community in a plural society; but in 2015, the church is an ex-majority minority community.

Vast minorities – but in two very different contexts seventeen centuries apart at the beginning and end of the Christendom era. Our focus will be on the Christian community in the early decades of the twenty-first century, the minority-that-used-to-be-a-majority that is struggling to adjust to this change of status, a vast minority that still has extraordinary resources if only these can be released and deployed in strategic and imaginative ways. But we will look back from time to time and learn from the vast minority that flourished for nearly three centuries before being co-opted into the empire. And we will find inspiration and receive insights from other minorities that challenged imperial Christianity and from Christians in other societies in which the Christian community has always been a minority.

There is nothing odd about Christians being in a minority. The Christendom era – in which the Christian community was an overwhelming majority throughout Europe and in other nations conquered and colonized by Europeans – was exceptional, not normative, despite lasting for so many centuries. And some of the legacies and vestiges of our majority status are problematic. We will need to identify these, assess their continuing impact, and consider how to deal with them as we continue to transition from this unusual majority status to the minority status that is the experience of most Christians. And, rather than indulging in nostalgia or succumbing to defeatism, we can choose to seize the many opportunities available to a vast minority – some of which a majority community would not have even recognized.

A note on terminology. 'Post-Christendom' is increasingly familiar as a way of describing the cultural transition through which Western societies are journeying, although in some circles this term is either unknown or confused with 'post-modernity'. Readers who are unfamiliar with this term can explore its meaning and implications in the popular and expanding 'After Christendom' series.[1] The Christian community's journey from majority to minority status is one aspect of this period.

The phrase 'vast minority' is used by others. Internet search engines point anyone interested to websites on a range of subjects:

---

[1] Since 2004, members of the Anabaptist Network have written books for this series, which is published by Paternoster. At the time of writing, seven had been published and seven more were under contract.

the term is used by anarchists anticipating the overthrow of capi-
talism; a heavy metal rock band; a site featuring amusing and
subversive photographs, cartoons and video clips; and several
sites challenging the under-representation of minority groups in
particular professions. Much closer to the use of the phrase in this
book is material on the Mennonite Trust's blog, 'A Vast Minority'
(http://avastminority.wordpress.com/).

And a note on the scope of this book. As will be evident, it
is concerned primarily with the challenges and opportunities
facing the Christian community in Britain. Data presented in
the following chapters relate to this community, and it is this
particular context that provides the backdrop to the subsequent
discussion. A very much longer and more complex book would be
required to explore the situation in other Western societies, in all
of which the Christian community is also now a vast minority, but
in each of which historical and cultural factors present different
scenarios. The United States of America is often regarded as an
exception, given the size and influence of its Christian community, but there is increasing evidence that this community is facing
similar challenges. Indeed, one of the very few books I have found
that explores the implications of a majority Christian community becoming a minority was written by an American church
leader and published as long ago as 1971.[2] In a remarkably pres-
cient series of lectures, Richard Koenig urged American churches
to prepare for minority status, identifying issues and offering
perspectives that over forty years later are relevant to the Christian community in many nations as we continue to grapple with
this transition. In no doubt that the huge Christian community in
America was inexorably moving from majority to minority status,
he encouraged his readers to believe that 'a small minority . . .
challenging the majority with a purer and more humane vision
possesses enormous force'.[3] Some of his insights will be integrated
into what follows.

The seven chapters in this book can be grouped into three short
sections. Chapters 1 and 2 map the dimensions of the 'vast minority'
and reflect on its prospects. Chapter 1 summarizes and interprets

---

[2]   Richard Edwin Koenig, *A Creative Minority: The Church in a New Age*
      (Minneapolis: Augsburg, 1971).
[3]   Koenig, *A Creative Minority*, p. 33.

the findings of censuses, polls and other forms of research, and explores some of the narratives of growth and decline that are offered by commentators. This is by far the most technical chapter and can be skipped or skim-read by readers with little interest in these details. Chapter 2 investigates the role and vocation of a minority Christian community in a society comprised of various minorities and identifies biblical resources to help us orientate ourselves in this context. Chapters 3 and 4 explore the potential of the Christian community as a 'vast minority', discuss what expectations it might nurture, consider adjustments that might enable it to fulfil its potential, and assess the resources and practices this community will need if it is to thrive. Chapters 5, 6 and 7 investigate the vocation of this 'vast minority', reflect on new opportunities that are becoming available, offer a theological and missional framework for action, and suggest that we might aspire to become a creative, prophetic and hopeful community.

1.

Minority Report

Counting Christians

How large is the Christian community in Britain today? This deceptively simple question is actually far from easy to answer. We need to consider several other questions before we can reach a meaningful conclusion. Some are to do with definition. How is membership in this community to be assessed? Who should be counted? And who decides? Others are to do with methodology. What measuring tools are appropriate? How accurate are the results? And how do we interpret various reports and studies?

As the title of this book indicates, like most others I believe that the Christian community is now a minority, albeit a sizeable one. But if we are to examine the implications of being a minority community in a plural society, some estimate of the size of this community will be a helpful starting point. Numbers are not everything, of course. The community's capacity is related at least as much to the depth of commitment, spiritual life, exercise of hospitality and missional orientation of its members. And there are wider issues, such as the extent to which the very mixed legacy of a supposedly Christianized culture remains influential and whether Christian faith perspectives are welcomed or excluded from public discourse. But we need some idea of the size of the Christian community.

Is this community a tiny minority or a very substantial minority? The difference might be numbered in millions, which will have huge consequences as we reflect on the community's role in society. And, despite the title of this book, is it, in fact, a minority or still a majority if measured in certain ways?

Affiliation

An obvious place to begin is the 2011 census. Every ten years the government collects and studies an enormous volume of information about the population. The data and documents analysing its meaning are released to the public and are used by academics, businesses, local authorities, government departments, churches and voluntary agencies to develop strategies, allocate resources and set priorities. Completing the census form is a legal requirement. For many decades religion had not featured in the census, but on the last two occasions, in 2001 and 2011, a question about religious affiliation was included. In 2011 the question asked was 'What is your religion?' Respondents were offered various boxes to tick and the opportunity to add any religion that was not listed. There was also a 'no religion' option.

Why was this question included? Perhaps until 2001 the religious affiliation of the overwhelming majority of the population was simply assumed to be Christian. Perhaps an increasingly secular society in the second half of the twentieth century was uninterested in this issue, assuming that religion was on the way out and did not need investigating. The initial response of the Office of National Statistics to the proposal from Churches Together in Britain and Ireland that such a question should be included in the 2001 census indicated this. But the campaign was successful. And perhaps by 2001 it was becoming clear that, despite the well-publicized decline in church membership, religion showed no signs of dying out in the near future, and the presence and growth of other faith communities in Britain meant that accurate information about the scope and diversity of religious affiliation was required.

Why was this question about religious affiliation the only optional question on the census form? If it was worth asking, why were we not required to answer it? Were those who framed the census of the opinion (long held in Britain) that religion is a private matter and squeamish about requiring us to reveal our convictions? In fact, only 7 per cent of the population declined to answer this question. There is no way of telling what difference their withheld answers might have made to the result. Were those who refused to answer less likely to be affiliated to a particular religion, inflating the 'no religion' category? Or did some highly committed members of various faith communities regard their affiliation as none of the state's business?

So what did the 2011 census reveal about the size of the Christian community? According to the information provided by respondents, 33.2 million people (59 per cent of the population) declared themselves to be Christians. If this is the appropriate measurement, the title of this book is wrong – Christians are still in the majority, albeit not as large a majority as ten years earlier when 72 per cent of the population declared themselves to be Christians. The loss of 4.1 million people from the Christian community during that decade is highly significant, of course, but its majority status persists.[1]

Cross-referencing this headline figure with other data gathered by the census reveals more about those who reported their affiliation to the Christian community:

- 22 per cent were aged sixty-five or older – a higher proportion than the overall population and the oldest age profile of the main religious groups. This was unchanged since 2001.
- 86 per cent were classified as White British but the proportion of respondents from minority ethnic backgrounds was higher than in 2001. The decrease in the Christian community since 2001 would have been 5.8 million if it had not been offset by the growth in ethnic minority Christian affiliation.
- 60 per cent of those reporting as Christians were economically inactive – the highest of any religious group and much higher than those reporting no religion – primarily because of retirement.

The census data also enables us to compare affiliation to the Christian community with other forms of religious affiliation. The second largest religious group was Muslims with nearly 5 per cent of the population (2.7 million people), up from 3 per cent a decade earlier. Their age profile was the youngest of the main religious groups. The most dramatic change, however, was in the proportion of people reporting no religious affiliation, up from 15 per cent in 2001 to 25 per cent (14.1 million people) in 2011. The age

[1] All the information in this section is taken from data on the website of the Office for National Statistics (http://www.ons.gov.uk).

profile of this group was significantly younger than the population as a whole and they were the most economically active group.

Whether information gathered in response to a census question about religious affiliation gives us an accurate picture of the size of the Christian community is doubtful. But this does not encourage any complacency about the persistence of majority status. If the decline continues at the same rate over the next decade, the headline figure will be under 50 per cent. If most of the 7 per cent who elected not to answer the question about religious affiliation have no such affiliation (as seems most likely), the 2011 figures suggest majority status is almost at an end already. The age profile of those declaring themselves Christians does not auger well for future trends. Although this has not changed much since 2001, those who are now at or beyond retirement age are the last generation with childhood memories of church and likely still to regard themselves as affiliated to the Christian community. And the level of economic inactivity among those affiliating to the Christian community implies diminishing financial resources.

But to what extent does this help us assess the size of the Christian community? How are we to interpret the data? The census asked nothing about believing, behaving or belonging. It asked only about religious affiliation. Did respondents identify themselves with a religion? It is surely legitimate to ask what this might mean and why people answered as they did, even if we cannot know for sure how to answer this question. Abby Day, senior research fellow at the University of Kent and advisor for the 2011 census on questions about religion, ethnicity and identity, suggests three categories of affiliation beyond those whose faith is 'integrated into their lives'. She differentiates between 'aspirational nominalists', who feel some affinity with the Christian faith, 'natal Christians', who regard their infant baptism as an identity marker, and 'ethnic Christians', who self-identify as Christians because they regard their British or other ethnic culture as Christian.[2]

Some have been utterly dismissive of this data, suggesting that it tells us nothing about the size of the Christian commu-

---

[2] Abby Day, 'Nominal Christian Adherence: Ethnic, Natal, Aspirational'. *Implicit Religion: Journal of the Centre for the Study of Implicit Religion and Contemporary Spirituality* 15/4 (2012), pp. 439–56.

nity. Pointing to the huge discrepancy between the proportion of the population claiming affiliation to Christianity and the much smaller proportion involved in any way in the churches, they conclude that the figure of 59 per cent is of no significance what-soever. Many British people, they argue, regularly declare them-selves to be 'Church of England' as a default position, whether or not they were christened in an Anglican church or have had any involvement with their parish church since. And as the census form offered 'Christian' rather than 'Church of England', this was the answer they gave.

Others have wondered whether this relatively high propor-tion of the population claiming to be Christians is a reaction to the presence and growing influence of other faith communities in Britain. Do at least some of the answers really mean 'not Muslim' or 'not Hindu'? Are they evidence that significant numbers of people, especially those aged sixty-five and over, feel discom-forted or threatened by a plural society? Is asserting Christian identity a response to this and an expression of nostalgia for a less diverse 'Christian nation'? Are these answers more about national or ethnic identity than religious affiliation? Our suspicion may deepen when we consider how the British National Party, for example, tries to co-opt Christianity for its own purposes. Its website speaks longingly of a time when 'the indigenous people' were 'united by their common Christian culture and heritage'.[3] Or it may simply be that, given Britain's Christian heritage, many people who believe in God but have no specifically Christian beliefs assume this means that they are Christians and declare themselves to be so.

Not all are inclined to dismiss the data or interpret it in these ways. Some find in it evidence of a continuing Christian majority, at least at the level of cultural identity. Writing before the 2011 data was fully available but reflecting on the 2001 census results and other more recent research, Roger Standing, principal of Spur-geon's College, London, writes: 'What these statistics demon-strate is an abiding cultural identification with Christianity. While it appears to be slowly diminishing at this point in history, it is still part of the self-identity of the overwhelming majority of the

[3] See http: / / www.bnp.org.uk / news / national / our-christian-tradi-tions-and-new-face-britain (accessed 11 Dec. 2013).

population.'[4] We will consider in due course the significance of such cultural identification, but it is clear from the 2011 census data that the majority is no longer 'overwhelming' and that this cultural identification has been diminishing rather more quickly since 2001.

Do other surveys confirm or challenge the findings of the 2011 census? Another recent source of information is the 2012 Integrated Household Survey, in which just over 400,000 people answered a question about religious affiliation. Of these, 68.5 per cent self-identified as Christian, substantially more than in the 2011 census, although the number of respondents was far smaller. The age profile was very similar to that revealed by the census, as were the percentages of those identifying as Muslims or having no religion. But the wording of the question was somewhat different from the census question: 'What is your religion, even if you are not currently practising?' Some commentators suggest that this question *assumes* a religious affiliation and so may have inflated the responses. Future IHS surveys will use the more neutral census question, making comparisons easier.

The annual British Social Attitudes Surveys ask, 'Do you regard yourself as belonging to any particular religion?'[5] The responses to this question are markedly different, perhaps because the wording implies that belonging to a religion is exceptional rather than normal. As long ago as 2009, only 45 per cent self-identified as Christians and a marginal majority of 51 per cent stated that they had no religious affiliation. Although the numbers interviewed were much smaller (only about 3,500), these figures support the findings of the 2011 census that affiliation to Christianity is continuing to wane. Whatever 'religious affiliation' means, we are unlikely to be able to claim for much longer that there is a Christian majority in Britain, even measured by this attenuated description.

Other surveys attempt to probe beyond religious affiliation in order to discover what those who claim to be Christians believe,

---

[4] Roger Standing, *As a Fire by Burning* (London: SCM Press, 2013), p. 182. *The Daily Mail* also reported on the basis of this research that 'the nation remains overwhelmingly Christian' (29 Sept. 2011).

[5] http://www.britsocat.com.

how they practise their faith and what involvement they have with the Christian community. These provide us with alternative measures for assessing the size and potential of the Christian community.

Believing

In September 2013 the polling and research agency ComRes conducted an online interview with just over two thousand adults that explored aspects of religious belief. The data they gathered, weighted to be representative of all adults in the country, formed the basis for an analysis and commentary by the think-tank, Theos, entitled 'The Spirit of Things Unseen: Belief in Post-Religious Britain'.[6]

This upbeat report celebrates the apparent persistence of what it calls 'a spiritual current' running through the nation and, while recognizing formalized religious belief has declined, asserts that 'the British have not become a nation of atheists or materialists'. Differentiating between 'religious' and 'spiritual' beliefs, the research indicates that substantial minorities of those interviewed believe in some kind of spiritual being, angels, life after death, the efficacy of prayer and the possibility of miracles. The report highlights the finding that 77 per cent of interviewees believe that 'there are things in life that we simply cannot explain through science or any other means'.

Critical commentators are less impressed, pointing out that 87 per cent do not believe in a personal god and 70 per cent do not believe in any kind of god, even defined in the vaguest way. The vast majority of people, it seems, do not believe in miracles or in the power of prayer, except in the sense that it makes the person praying feel more peaceful. The meaning of 'spirituality' in the research and the subsequent report is very much attenuated, but even so only just over half the interviewees admit to any spiritual beliefs.[7] And research by Michael King, professor of psychiatry at University College, London, in the same year revealed that only 20 per cent of people described themselves as 'spiritual'.[8]

[6] http://www.theosthinktank.co.uk/publications/2013/10/17/the-spirit-of-things-unseen-belief-in-post-religious-britain.

[7] A brief analysis of this report appears in *Third Way* 36/10 (2013), p. 21.

[8] See further *Vista* 16 (2014), p. 7.

We cannot engage here with the ongoing debate about whether Britain is becoming steadily more secular or whether residual religious beliefs and various emerging forms of spirituality mean that our society should be designated 'post-secular'. For our purposes, the significance of this research lies in what it tells us about the beliefs *of those who claim to be Christians*. If this small sample is truly representative, there is a worrying discrepancy between the census data, in which 59 per cent of the population claimed Christian affiliation, and the data in this survey, in which 87 per cent do not believe in a personal god. Indeed, it appears that only 62 per cent of those claiming to be Christians 'think that spiritual forces have some influence on either people's thoughts, events in the human world, or events in the natural world'.[9]

At the very least, this research suggests that there is a large gap between Christian affiliation and belief in the most basic tenets of the Christian faith. While respecting the desire of many to self-identify as Christians in the 2011 census, we are surely unwise to measure the scope and potential of the Christian community without reference to their beliefs.

Earlier in 2013 YouGov carried out a wide-ranging survey among young adults (18- to 24-year-olds) and in June reported their findings. Answers to questions relating to religious affiliation and religious beliefs revealed that 28 per cent claimed Christian affiliation – less than half the figure in the 2011 census – and only 25 per cent believed in God (with a further 19 per cent saying they believed in 'some sort of spiritual greater power', but not God). Not only does this research indicate that Christian affiliation is much more limited among young adults, so that the next census is highly unlikely to find even a bare majority claiming to be Christians; it underlines the concern raised above that affiliation and belief are by no means equivalent. If most of the 10 per cent in the survey who claimed affiliation to other religions do believe in God, then it appears that a significant proportion of the few young adults who self-identify as Christians do not actually believe in God.

These surveys are not exceptional. A number of others in recent years have reported similar findings. Another YouGov poll in 2011 of sixty-four thousand representative British adults discovered

[9] From the Theos report; see Note 9 above.

that 34 per cent believed in a personal (theist) or non-intervening (deist) God and another 10 per cent in a generic 'higher power'. A *Financial Times* Harris Poll conducted in November and December 2006 revealed that of the 12,500 people were polled, only 35 per cent believed in any kind of God or supreme being. A poll carried out by *New Scientist* in 2003 found that 55 per cent did not believe in a 'higher being'. And in a Mori Poll in the same year, only 55 per cent could name even one of the four gospels. Comparing the results of many surveys in the previous fifty years, Robin Gill, professor of applied theology at the University of Kent, concluded in 2003 that Christian beliefs had been steadily declining over this much longer period.[10]

A number of commentators have followed the lead of sociologist Grace Davie in asserting that in Britain many 'believe without belonging'.[11] Monica Furlong interpreted the situation similarly in her review of the Church of England in 2000.[12] However, there is increasing evidence that this is no longer the case. Rather than believing without belonging, many neither belong nor believe. Furthermore, it is not clear how deeply any remaining beliefs are held or whether these beliefs have any impact on the way people live. These are not issues most surveys address, but research commissioned by the British Library in 2007 concluded that half of those who claimed to have religious beliefs did not practise these 'very much if at all', with those claiming to be Christians apparently the most inactive.

David Voas, professor of population studies at the University of Essex, questions how much credence can be given to what people say to pollsters when asked about their beliefs. He points to research that suggests people feel obliged to express opinions on such matters but that their views are 'uninformed, not deeply held, seldom acted upon and relatively volatile'. He calls this 'believing without believing' and warns: 'we cannot conclude from the fact that people tell pollsters they believe in God that

[10] Robin Gill, 'Measuring Church Trends over Time', in *Public Faith?* (ed. Paul Avis; London: SPCK, 2003), p. 25.

[11] Grace Davie, *Religion in Britain since 1945: Believing without Belonging* (Oxford: Blackwell, 1994).

[12] Monica Furlong, *C of E: The State It's In* (London: Hodder & Stoughton, 2000).

they give the matter any thought, find it significant, will feel the same next year, or plan to do anything about it.'[13]

Whether Christian affiliation or Christians' beliefs are being measured, research indicates that both have been declining over many decades. Those who self-identify as Christians *may* still be a marginal majority, although probably not for much longer, but those who hold even the most basic Christian beliefs have been a minority for some time and currently comprise only a small proportion of those who claim Christian affiliation. This reality must be taken into account in any attempt to assess the size of the Christian community.

Belonging

What we often mean, of course, when speaking about the size of the Christian community is the number of people involved in some way in the roughly fifty thousand churches in Britain. Rather than the vague notion of Christian affiliation or the confusing findings of research into what people say they believe, we are interested in the question of belonging. And it is here that the discrepancy between different ways of measuring the Christian community becomes most apparent.

Belonging is itself a contested term. What counts as belonging? How frequently does one need to attend to be registered? Does it matter whether participation is active or largely passive? Is membership a more or less reliable indicator than attendance? Measuring any of these expressions of belonging has become increasingly difficult as denominations have proliferated and forms of church have multiplied and diversified. The major denominations employ very different ways of measuring attendance or membership. Not all churches keep records. Many are invisible to researchers if they have no public meeting places or offices. So veteran researcher Peter Brierley acknowledges[14] that 'membership is a composite term, an inexact term in its cumulation', but insists that it 'gives . . . a firmer indication of religious commitment than just ticking a box saying "Christian" on a census or other form'.

---

[13] David Voas, 'Is Britain a Christian Country?' in Avis, *Public Faith*, p. 96.

[14] See http://www.brierleyconsultancy.com/images/csintro.pdf, p. 1.

The most frequently referenced and widely respected research into the question of belonging is the 2005 English Church Census, carried out on 8 May 2005 by Christian Research.[15] This involved approximately half of the known churches in England and the results were adjusted to take into account estimates of churches that did not participate, drawing on published data about those churches. As we ponder the findings of this census, four caveats should be borne in mind. First, this information is now several years old and so needs to be treated with some caution. Second, the census only involved 'known' churches in its findings and estimates, but in some contexts many 'unknown' churches might have added significantly to the outcomes. Third, the census measured attendance on a specific Sunday and so did not take into account churches meeting on other days of the week or Christians participating in other ways in those churches that were included. Fourth, the census took place only in England and so does not include information about the rest of Britain.

From the wealth of information provided by the census, we note here some findings that are of particular interest:

- Non-White church attendance had increased by 19 per cent since 1998, while White church attendance had dropped by 19 per cent. Few observers doubt that this trend has continued since 2005, especially in London and other cities, changing the face of the English churches.
- The combined total of 'Free Church' attenders was larger than either the Anglican or Catholic totals, which were roughly equivalent to each other, implying that the status of the Church of England as the national church and the default affiliation of English people is under serious threat.
- Within the overall picture of decline can be found areas of growth. Pentecostals, for instance, had experienced a 34 per cent rise in attendance since 1998 and Orthodox churches had grown by 2 per cent.
- Within particular denominations there had also been changes in the composition of church attenders with, for instance, an

[15] http://www.christian-research.org. More information and analysis can be found in Peter Brierley, *Pulling out of the Nosedive* (London: Christian Research, 2006).

increasing proportion of evangelicals in some and a decreasing proportion in others. Across the board, evangelicals represented an increased proportion of a declining church.

The headline figure derived from the census was that 6.3% of the population of England (a little over 3 million people) could be regarded as regular church attenders in 2005. This represented a 15 per cent decline since the previous census in 1998. If this level of decline has continued since 2005, the size of the Christian community, if measured by regular attendance, will be considerably reduced. Data collected subsequently by Peter Brierley, this time directly from denominations, rather than from a church census, indicates that it has.[16] Recently, he has reported figures indicating church attendance in England was 5.5% in 2013.[17] In other words, the pattern and rate of decline over the past fifty years is continuing.

Another resource that attempted to measure belonging in terms of attendance but did so in a rather different way was 'Church-going in the UK', a report by Tearfund published in 2007.[18] As the title indicates, this report included other parts of Britain as well as England, and one of its unsurprising findings was that attendance was much higher in Northern Ireland, slightly higher in Scotland and slightly lower in Wales than in England. We should, of course, bear in mind that this research is also now several years old and so needs to be treated with caution, not only in relation to its headline figures but also in relation to the regional differences it reported. The most significant difference, however, was not between regions but in the way in which this report measured attendance. Weddings, baptisms, funerals and other invitation-only events were excluded, but all 'voluntary attendance' at events on any day of the week in a church building was included. Not surprisingly, this resulted in a considerably higher figure than that derived only two years earlier from the English Church Census. Ten per cent of the population (4.9 million people), rather than 6.3 percent, are regarded as weekly attenders.

[16] See http://www.brierleyconsultancy.com/images/csintro.pdf, p. 5.

[17] See Peter Brierley, 'Church Decline put back by 5 Years', *Future First* 33 (2014).

[18] See http://www.whychurch.org.uk/tearfund_church.pdf.

However, the report suggested that monthly attendance should be regarded as normative and concluded that 15 per cent of the population (7.6 million people) were regular attenders. If those it designated as 'fringe' and 'occasional' attenders were added, this would amount to 26 per cent of the population (12.6 million) attending at least annually. The discrepancy between the figures given in this report and the findings of the English Church Census illustrates the difficulty of defining 'attendance', let alone what it really means to 'belong' to the Christian community. Add to this the different ways of measuring adopted by different denominations (the Church of England, for example, has included weddings and funerals in their weekly attendance statistics since 2000) and questions about the relationship between attendance and membership (figures for these categories sometimes move in opposite directions within the same denomination), and the notion of belonging becomes ever more complex.

Researchers have also noted the possibility that interviewees might overstate their attendance. In societies where there is still a degree of cultural pressure, or at least social acceptability, about church attendance, this can be a serious problem. Some researchers in the United States have worried that self-declared church attendance rates might be as much as twice as high as the reality. This may be less problematic in Britain, where some people might deny attending church even if they do, especially if interviewed in public, because of the stigma attached to such an activity, but some researchers have detected inflated claims in relation to both belief and attendance.

A further complication is the emergence of 'fresh expressions of church' within several major denominations and how to count those who are involved in these. Most contain a substantial number who also attend a more traditional form of church, so these should not be double-counted in any research. But many also attend who do not belong to other forms of church and who may not (or not yet) regard themselves as Christians. So should only those who have become Christians within these fresh expressions of church and do not attend any other form of church be counted? The Church of England reports that its researchers are 'adapting the annual church attendance counts to include attendance at fresh expressions of church and also beginning to monitor attendance at chapels in universities and other places of worship.

The growing ministry of chaplains in shopping centres, hospitals and other places has yet to be numerically reflected.'[19]

Careful diocese-by-diocese research undertaken by the Church Army's research unit during 2012 and 2013 has begun to clarify the situation in relation to Anglican 'fresh expressions of church'. Although the initial report released in January 2014 was based on research into only ten dioceses, this indicated that a quarter of those attending were already church members, a third used to be church members and 40 per cent had no previous church background.[20] Other dioceses are currently being researched, so more information may soon be available.

Much more numerous than those involved in these fresh expressions of church but also hard to quantify are Christians belonging to the many African, Asian, Latin American, Caribbean and other culturally specific churches that have flourished and multiplied in recent years. In these cases there is little doubt about the level of commitment involved, although there are aspects of cultural Christianity in some of these communities, and attendance is often much more regular than in other churches. The difficulty here is discovering and then keeping track of churches that emerge, move to new venues, divide and multiply, and may have no formal membership and little interest in keeping attendance records. But these churches represent a vibrant and increasingly numerous section of the Christian community.

The other constituency we must consider as we attempt to estimate the scope of the Christian community is those who self-identify as Christians, hold orthodox Christian beliefs and are committed to Christian discipleship and Christian witness, but who do not (or no longer) belong to any particular church. The exodus over recent years of many church members is well documented, as are the reasons why they left. Although some only ever attended for family or cultural reasons and others are moving away from the Christian beliefs they once held, many others remain deeply committed to Christ.[21]

---

[19] http://www.churchofengland.org/media/1477827/2010_11church-statistics.pdf, p. 2.

[20] See http: // www.freshexpressions.org.uk / news / anglicanresearch. See also http://www.churchgrowthresearch.org.uk/report.

[21] See Stuart Murray, *Church after Christendom* (Milton Keynes: Paternoster, 2004), pp. 39–56.

This group is sometimes lumped together under the term 'de-churched', as distinct from the 'unchurched', who have never professed to be Christian or attended church. According to the Tearfund report, this group is twice the size of those who attend church regularly and might comprise 33 per cent of the population (over 16 million people). But this figure and the catch-all category of 'de-churched' are not at all helpful. As we think about the scope and capacity of the Christian community, those who continue as followers of Jesus without the support of church involvement (however we assess the wisdom of this) must not be conflated with those who have abandoned their faith, those who had attended church without believing, or those who merely claim Christian affiliation. And some researchers predict that a growing number of Christians may interpret 'belonging' in other ways than local church membership. Helen Cameron, founding director and research fellow of the Oxford Centre for Ecclesiology and Practical Theology, suggests that 'by 2050, of those describing themselves as actively involved in the church only about one-quarter will be members of a local church'. The rest will be involved in so-called para-church organizations, campaigning organizations or networks of informal small groups.[22]

Who counts?

If we are to offer any meaningful answer to the question with which we opened this chapter – how large is the Christian community? – we will need to decide who counts. There are two issues here: who does the counting and who is counted in or out of the Christian community?

As we have seen, researchers investigate various ways of counting the Christian community. We have summarized findings in relation to affiliation, belief and belonging, but we could have investigated ideology, morality, ritual (how many have been baptized or confirmed?), behaviour and practice (for example, who prays?). The results vary enormously, not least because researchers ask subtly different questions or investigate different

---

[22] Helen Cameron, 'The Decline of the Church in England as a Local Membership Organization: Predicting the Nature of Civil Society in 2050', in *Predicting Religion* (ed. Grace Davie, Paul Heelas and Linda Woodhead; Aldershot: Ashgate, 2003), p. 118.

constituencies, so we need to decide which of these approaches, or which combination of approaches, is most helpful as we assess the scope of the community. And this is where our assumptions, vested interests and theological convictions come into play. We may have reasons for embracing a restrictive estimate of the size of the Christian community or a more generous one.

Those with very clear ideas of what Christians must believe or of which churches represent authentic Christianity may dismiss much of the research as irrelevant and conclude that the 'true' Christian community is tiny. Some would argue that it always has been and, indeed, always will be. Faithfulness, they argue, matters much more than size – and faithfulness is equated with those whose beliefs and practices are more or less the same as those doing the counting. Some Protestants and Pentecostals, for example, will discount all Catholics. Some evangelicals will discount those with more liberal theological perspectives.

On the other hand, those who remain committed to the public and cultural role of the church in an increasingly plural society, and who campaign for the continuation of its social influence and legal privileges, are likely to resist attempts to measure the Christian community in ways that diminish its size and weaken its claims. Anglicans, especially, who remain committed to the notion of a state church with a national mandate, are liable to adopt very generous methods of measuring the Christian community. This tendency is evident throughout the otherwise very helpful collection of essays edited by Paul Avis, *Public Faith?* This book, published in 2003, identifies several flaws in research into the size of the Christian community, warning against drawing definitive conclusions from the kind of evidence surveyed in this chapter, but several writers advocate approaches that unrealistically enhance the size of the community (although they accept that it is shrinking, whatever measurements are used).

As we ponder these divergent approaches within the churches to counting Christians, it might be helpful to ask how others see us. Who do politicians, sociologists, humanists, Muslims and members of the media count as Christians? Not that those outside the Christian community are any less influenced by presuppositions and ulterior motives, but perspectives from outside might bring fresh insights to bear.

For some years now, politicians have preferred the term 'faith communities' to differentiating between specific religious groups, as have developers when allocating sacred spaces in new housing areas. This not only avoids the need for multiple conversations with representatives of different religious communities; it also serves the interests of a secular mainstream culture that prefers to homogenize and marginalize all religious groups. Some may still affirm, when pressed, that Britain is a 'Christian nation' or has a 'Christian heritage', and most public religious ceremonies are still overwhelmingly Christian in their orientation and participation. But these statements and occasions owe more to the past status of Christianity than to its continuing majority affiliation in the population.

And they are now routinely and robustly challenged, as was evident in April 2014 when fifty public figures wrote an open letter objecting strongly to the Prime Minister, David Cameron's claim that Britain was 'a Christian country'. This provoked an interesting public debate for a few days, with some church leaders clamouring to endorse this claim, representatives of the National Secular Society pouring scorn on these 'self-serving' and deluded endorsements, and more measured responses recognizing both the country's 'Christian heritage' and the much more diverse reality today.[23]

Actually, when the media carry stories about what Christians say or do, whether these reports are positive or negative, they certainly do not mean that the persons or organizations involved are among the 59 per cent who claimed to be Christians on the census forms. In the media, the term 'Christian' is almost invariably used in a much more restrictive sense. Sometimes, in the recent past, the terms 'born again' or 'committed' were added to clarify this, but these terms appear to have become redundant. 'Christian' is now enough in most cases. This usage might encourage us to adopt a similarly more restrictive measure as we estimate the extent of the Christian community.

This debate could continue indefinitely, but we need to reach at least a tentative conclusion if we are to explore the implications for the Christian community in Britain today. The title of this

[23] See http://www.bbc.co.uk/news/uk-27099700 and subsequent news reports.

book points towards such a conclusion and in the Introduction a specific figure is suggested: 10 per cent of the population. This is much smaller than the percentage claiming in surveys to be Christians. It is also fewer than those holding vague theistic or spiritual beliefs. But it is significantly higher than the best estimate of those who belong to local churches and attend regularly, as it takes into account at least some of those who do not participate in these churches but retain recognizably Christian beliefs that impact the way they live.

This conclusion will not satisfy everyone reading this chapter. Some will regard it as overly restrictive and even judgemental. Others will regard it as too generous, embracing those who attend churches but do not subscribe to fundamental Christian beliefs or practise their faith in any other way. But a Christian community that comprises 10 per cent of the population is the 'vast minority' with which we will be concerned in what lies ahead. This is very definitely a minority. But it is a sizeable community of around six million people – a community with huge resources of money and time, infrastructure, organizational capacity, community engagement, social capital and buildings. What might be its vocation in a society where it is no longer the majority? And how might it re-imagine itself and deploy its resources most effectively?

Narratives of Decline and Growth

Before we explore the vocation and potential of the Christian community, however, we need to assess not only its current dimensions but also its future prospects. Whether the proposed figure of 10 per cent of the population is too high, too low or a reasonable estimate, we need to know whether the community is declining, stable or growing. If it is still declining, we need to ask whether it can sustain its current level of activity, let alone take on new challenges, whereas a growing community might plan for fresh initiatives with some measure of confidence.

Nobody disputes that the Christian community has been declining in size and influence over the past several decades. The 2011 census and other surveys differ in specifics but agree that the overall trend is downwards, whether they are measuring affiliation, belief or belonging. It seems that the number who believe without belonging is diminishing, the number who belong without believing is diminishing, and the number who neither belong nor believe is growing. But is this decline likely to continue? If so, will the rate of decline decrease or accelerate? Or are there signs of stabilization or even growth in the Christian community?

The narrative of decline has undoubtedly been dominant, in the churches and in the writings of social commentators. In 2009, Christian Research predicted that in 2050 there will be just 3,600 Methodists left in Britain and only 4,400 Presbyterians. Projecting forward the current rate of decline in some denominations has produced a date in the 2030s or 2040s when these denominations will no longer have any churches or any members at all. The Methodists, the United Reformed Church, the Church of Scotland, the Church in Wales and the Salvation Army are all facing this prospect.[24] Nobody is actually suggesting that these denominations will become extinct at that point, but these are salutary projections and imply that, at the very least, these parts of the Christian community will have diminishing capacity and limited resources over the next two decades.

Furthermore, their institutional structures will become unsustainable and will necessitate staff cuts and simplified ways of operating. A senior leader in one of these denominations told me recently (in a private conversation) that their money will run out as soon as 2017! In some of these denominations, of course, decline increases the funds available as redundant church buildings are sold to developers, but this is a temporary phenomenon and is not particularly helpful unless these additional resources are deployed in transformative ways. Funding shortages and organizational restructuring are evident in other denominations too, including the Baptist Union of Great Britain, which has not experienced the same level of decline.

Particular difficulties, institutional and emotional, are facing the Anglicans, especially in England. For so long the dominant part of the Christian community in England and officially still the 'established' church, Church of England congregations now constitute less than one third of those who attend churches.

---

[24] For sources, see Stuart Murray, *Post-Christendom* (Carlisle: Paternoster, 2004), p. 6.

Within what is already a minority Christian community, Anglicans now represent a minority within this minority. This is one aspect of the reshaping and diversifying of the Christian community. Colin Marsh, ecumenical development officer of Birmingham Churches Together, writes: 'In the same way that Birmingham is becoming a majority minority city, so too the Christian community will continue to diversify and present day minorities may well form the majority of the Christian community in the next decade.'[25]

Furthermore, although most Anglicans remain strongly committed to 'national coverage' through the parish system, this system is being stretched to breaking point as parish priests are frequently required to operate within vast areas of conjoined parishes. The diocese of Monmouth, part of the Church in Wales, is the first Anglican diocese to acknowledge that this is unsustainable. Since 2013 it has been transitioning from parish ministry to 'ministry areas'.[26] Although this is being presented as a basis for growth and clergy are being retrained for missional ministry, declining numbers and reduced financial resources have necessitated this process. Other dioceses may follow suit.

While there is no definite evidence yet that the Christian community has arrested its decline, there have been indications that the rate of decline has slowed in recent years. Peter Brierley, in his interpretation of the findings of the 2005 English Church Census, employed the image of 'pulling out of the nosedive'. Pointing to various signs of hope and to evidence that some aspects of decline were less dramatic than in the previous census in 1998, he concluded that 'the church is not inexorably destined to die'. By comparison with the image used in his previous book,[27] 'the tide is running out', this sounds like good news. But Brierley warned against complacency. 'No levelling out is in sight yet,' he wrote, so the church 'still has to pull out of the nosedive fully if it is to become airborne again', adding: 'It is always possible to

---

[25] Colin Marsh, 'The Diversification of English Christianity: The Example of Birmingham', in *Church Growth in Britain 1980 to the Present* (ed. David Goodhew; Farnham: Ashgate, 2012), p. 194.

[26] See http://monmouth.churchinwales.org.uk/ministry-areas/.

[27] Peter Brierley, *The Tide is Running Out* (London: Christian Research, 2000).

nosedive a second time.'[28] He anticipated continuing decline from 6.3 per cent in 2005 to 5.1 per cent in 2015 and 4.5 per cent in 2020. His successor as director of Christian Research, Benita Hewitt, commenting on figures collated in 2010, was more sanguine: 'At long last it looks as if we may be reaching the end of the decline of church attendance in the UK.'[29] But this may be precipitate, or at least applicable only to England. Extrapolating from information showing a 6 per cent rate of decline between 2005 and 2010 (very close to earlier predictions), Brierley has predicted a similar rate of decline between 2010 and 2015. The English figures may be static, but further decline in Wales, Scotland and Northern Ireland means that overall decline in UK churches is likely to persist, even if this rate is not increasing.[30]

A slowing rate of decline is not surprising, even without the signs of hope and growth noted by Brierley and others (which we will explore below). Although sustained decline over many years has precipitated church closures and will continue to do so, accompanied probably by some denominational disintegration, what remains may be a hard core of vibrant churches and highly committed people who are resilient and effective in expanding their communities. It is possible that the decline in the Christian community might constitute a kind of pruning that could lead to stronger churches and prospects for sustainable growth. As Roger Standing writes, many denominational leaders 'report that they have many growing congregations and that the present overall decline is produced by a more rapid falling away of those churches that are in difficulty. The underlying health of the growing churches means that at some point in the future a different scenario will become apparent.'[31] He concludes: 'The narrative of the decline of Christianity, the closing of churches and the ageing of believers is true, but only in part . . . To be hostage to the narrative of decline and irrelevance leads to an embattled and dispirited mindset that saps energy and quenches creativity. But this would involve being hostage to a lie.'[32]

---

[28] Brierley, *Pulling out of the Nosedive*, p. vi.

[29] 'Churchgoing Numbers More Stable'. *Quadrant* 23 (2010), pp. 1–2.

[30] See http://www.brierleyconsultancy.com/images/csintro.pdf, p. 5.

[31] Standing, *As a Fire by Burning*, p. 181.

[32] Standing, *As a Fire by Burning*, p. 184.

How many congregations are growing? According to the 2005 English Church Census, just over one third (34 per cent) of churches in England grew in the seven years since the previous census. An Anglican report released in January 2014 estimated that, in the decade up to 2010, 18 per cent of churches grew; 55 per cent remained stable and 27 per cent declined.[33] Within the overall picture of continuing, if decelerating, decline, these are encouraging findings. This narrative of growth needs to be read alongside the narrative of decline, especially if results from the next census reveal a similar picture. Even if these growing congregations are not yet growing enough to offset the overall decline, at some point they might, in which case the Christian community will indeed have pulled out of its nosedive. In addition, over the past thirty years in Britain a new church has been planted on average almost every day. Even though almost as many have closed and not all the newly planted churches have thrived, this is encouraging, not least because many new churches will be healthier and more engaged with their surrounding culture than those that closed.[34]

Narratives of growth in the Christian community need to be read with both enthusiasm and caution. After decades of decline, it is understandable that any signs of growth are welcomed with open arms, but we must not allow these to lull us into a false sense of security. They do not mean that the long decline has ended or is now in reverse, much less that we are no longer a minority community. The exuberant response to a recent book identifying signs of growth in the past thirty years made for potent headlines in the Christian media but failed to reflect the more measured tone of its editor. As David Goodhew of Cranmer Hall, Durham, writes in the introduction to *Church Growth in Britain: 1980 to the Present*, the aim of this book was 'not to airbrush out . . . wholesale church decline in recent decades' but to 'highlight sides of the story which have been hitherto marginalized'. As such, it focuses on examples of growth, but Goodhew warns: 'Such developments are no cause

---

[33] See http://www.churchofengland.org/media/1909677/church-growth-report-review3.pdf, p. 12.

[34] See the more detailed analysis at http://www.brierleyconsultancy.com/images/ff22.pdf.

for ecclesiastical triumphalism, given the extent of church decline elsewhere.'[35]

Nevertheless, these examples of growth are encouraging and might, if they are sustained and proliferate, result in the Christian community stabilizing and even beginning to grow instead of continuing to decline in the decades ahead. Contributors from England, Scotland, Wales and Northern Ireland and from Catholic, Anglican and Free Church traditions reflect on the significance of growth in such areas as cathedral attendance, fresh expressions of church, the Black churches and various mainstream congregations. The 2014 report on Anglican 'fresh expressions of church' indicated that the rate at which fresh expressions are starting increased rapidly between 2010 and 2012, and that overall attendance was equivalent to a whole new diocese.[36] These may be instances of what one contributor refers to as 'growth amidst decline', but they challenge the prevailing narrative of relentless decline and the inertia and discouragement that narrative produces. Similarly, in his General Secretary's report to the Methodist Conference in 2013, Martyn Atkins commented that 'the information coming from our Statistics for Mission in respect of fresh expressions of church is hugely encouraging', even though he rightly set this news in the context of continuing denominational decline.[37]

What Goodhew's book does not offer, however, is a prescription for growth. The examples it gives are very different from each other and engage with different sectors of society. There is, it seems, no simple or single strategy that will arrest or reverse decades of decline. This point is underscored by one of the researchers of the 2014 Anglican report, which provided further evidence of growth in cathedral congregations and fresh expressions of church. David Voas warns that 'there is no single recipe for growth; there are no simple solutions to decline. The road to growth depends on the context, and what works in one place may not work in another.'[38]

---

[35] David Goodhew, ed., *Church Growth in Britain: 1980 to the Present* (Farnham: Ashgate, 2012), pp. 3–4.

[36] See http://www.freshexpressions.org.uk/news/anglicanresearch.

[37] See http://methodist.org.uk/conference/conference-reports/ 2013-reports.

[38] http://www.churchofengland.org/media/1909677/church-growth-report-review3.pdf, p. 5.

Another recent book that contributes to the narrative of growth is Peter Brierley's report on the findings of the 2012 London Church Census.[39] It has been apparent for some time that, in church attendance as in many other ways, London is different from the rest of the country. The census found that between 2005 and 2012 church attendance in the capital increased by a remarkable 16 per cent. In 2012, 9 per cent of Londoners were in church, as compared to the national average of about 6 per cent. The number of places of worship in London also rose during these seven years, by 17 per cent from 4,100 to 4,800. Brierley reflects on the main factors, not least the growth of the Black churches and the impact of Pentecostalism, and highlights mechanisms that might be relevant in other cities. In other regions, too, there is clear evidence of growth among Pentecostals.

Prospects

Cross-referencing the narratives of decline and growth, the prospects for the near future of the Christian community in Britain are uncertain.[40] Many more congregations are likely to disappear, but many new congregations and fresh expressions of church will be planted. It is likely that some denominations will disintegrate or survive only by merging with others. If growing churches can continue to grow and reproduce themselves, rather than stagnating and losing their missional focus, there could be overall growth within the next twenty years. But the rate at which many congregations are ageing and the seeming indifference or hostility of the younger generation towards the Christian faith present major challenges. The capacity of Black and other ethnic minority churches to grow beyond their own constituency might be a critical component in all this, as the phenomenon of 'reverse mission'

[39] Peter Brierley, *Capital Church Growth* (London: ADBC Publishers, 2014).
[40] The focus throughout this book is on Britain, but similar statistics and trends can be discerned in most other Western nations. Even in America, often regarded as an exception, similar trends are becoming evident, albeit the Christian community is still much larger and more influential.

grows in significance and as second- and third-generation leaders explore ways of engaging more effectively with others in a plural society. And the growth and increasing influence of Islam and other faith communities might result in further attrition from the Christian community or possibly in its growth as members of a post-secular society grapple afresh with issues of religion.

What is not seriously in question is that the Christian community in Britain will be a minority for the foreseeable future. It will most likely continue to decline for some years yet, albeit at a slower rate than in recent years, but there will be instances of growth and signs of hope that at some point this decline will end and give way to a period of stability or even overall growth. But, however the dynamics of growth and decline interact, there is no realistic prospect of the Christian community becoming anything other than a minority for many decades.

Our concern in the rest of this book is not to delve more deeply into the statistics or to reflect further on the competing narratives of decline and growth, but to ask how the Christian community can live well as a 'vast minority'. What is required if we are to make the difficult journey from perceived majority status to acknowledged minority status? What can we no longer do, and what can we now do that we could not before? What roles can we play in a plural society? And what do we need to sustain ourselves and our communities?

2.

Minorities and Majorities

From Majority to Minority

There is nothing unusual or extraordinary about the Christian community in Britain being a minority in a plural culture. In many parts of the world over the past twenty centuries, this has been the status and experience of Christians.

Sometimes the Christian community has been very small, statistically insignificant. At other times it has been much more substantial and has had the capacity and opportunities to make a significant impact on the rest of society. In some contexts it has been an oppressed and persecuted minority; in others, it has been tolerated or even valued and protected from discrimination. And in every context, including first-century Judaea, the Christian community began as a minority, even if in some places and in some periods it achieved majority status.

Indeed, if we remove our Eurocentric blinkers and survey the church through the centuries and around the globe, we might conclude that situations in which the Christian community enjoys majority status are exceptional. The Christian community in Europe achieved this status during the fourth and fifth centuries and maintained this throughout the next fifteen centuries, but the Christian community in Asia, planted by missionaries who went east from Jerusalem, rather than west, may have outnumbered the European church during the medieval period but never achieved majority status. For several centuries it was a vast minority within societies dominated by Zoroastrians, Hindus, Buddhists and Muslims.

European Christianity was exported and often imposed on other cultures, as missionaries and soldiers accompanied adventurers and merchants to the Americas. There was no question that this transplanted European Christianity would supplant indigenous belief systems and achieve majority status. In Australasia, too, the settlers brought with them assumptions that required a majority-status Christian community and the suppression of aboriginal cultures. But in Africa and Asia, with few exceptions (such as Nagaland in India or among tribal groups such as the Karen in Thailand), the Christian community has not achieved majority status. It may yet do so if the phenomenal growth of the Christian community in some societies, especially in sub-Saharan Africa, continues. But for most African and Asian Christians, today and throughout the centuries, their experience has been within minority communities.[1]

This means that there are resources on which we can draw as we explore the implications of being a minority community today. There are Christian communities all over the world from which we can learn if we have the humility to do so. Our history and culture are not the same as theirs, but their experiences of living as minority communities can inspire and help us.

However, we need to sound a note of caution before equating these contexts. What is unusual about the status of the Christian community in Britain and other Western societies is that it is a minority that *used to be a majority*. There are many historical examples of the Christian community moving from minority to majority status, but fewer examples of moving from majority to minority. This transition, which has taken place over the past several decades, presents a range of challenges that are different from those facing Christian communities that have never been majorities. Richard Koenig writes: 'Because of their past success Christians today are ill-prepared to live in a world which contradicts their most cherished ambitions and regards them as irrelevant. This defeat-from-the-jaws-of-victory feeling makes contemporary Christian

---

[1] Some of these minority communities are, of course, vast. Some dwarf their Western counterparts, such as the 17 million Anglicans in Nigeria as against about 1 million in Britain, reminding us that the Christian community in Britain is not only a minority of the British population but also a minority in the world church.

experience one of the most poignant in the church's history.'[2] To the theological, psychological, institutional and missional implications involved we will shortly turn.

First, though, we may need to qualify the claim that the Christian community in Britain is an ex-majority minority and acknowledge that there are different perspectives on this.

Was the Christian community in Britain or in the rest of Europe ever truly a majority community? How Christian was the culture historians call 'Christendom'? Undoubtedly, the vast majority of Europeans would have identified themselves as Christians and would have asserted, if asked, that they lived in a Christian society. There were minorities – the Jewish community, Muslims in the south of Europe and those often described as 'freethinkers', who did not believe what the vast majority believed. But if it took courage in the centuries before Constantine to be a Christian, it took courage in the Christendom era *not* to be a Christian. Minorities frequently suffered discrimination and persecution from the majority Christian community, but they persisted. Christendom was not uniform, even if it was overwhelmingly Christian.

What did it mean, though, to be a Christian in those centuries? Some historians have probed the cultures of communities across Europe and have concluded that many pagan beliefs and practices survived for centuries after Europe became officially Christian. Sometimes these were suppressed or forced underground, but often they flourished alongside Christian beliefs and practices, leading some historians to suggest that Christendom was nothing more than a thin veneer of Christianity superimposed on older paganism. Church historian Kenneth Scott Latourette writes: 'The experience of thoroughgoing moral and spiritual renewal was probably shared by only a minority of Christians.'[3] Other historians have noted that, despite church attendance being legally required during the Christendom era, the actual level of attendance varied enormously and was often remarkably low. And in an era when parish priests were often uneducated and profoundly ignorant of even basic Christian beliefs, and when churchgoing

---

[2] Richard Edwin Koenig, *A Creative Minority: The Church in a New Age* (Minneapolis: Augsburg, 1971), p. 29.

[3] Kenneth Scott Latourette, *The First Five Centuries* (Grand Rapids: Zondervan, 1970), p. 167.

was almost entirely passive, how can we assess the level of belief and practice?[4] Andrew Greeley concludes, more bluntly than most: 'There could be no de-Christianization of Europe . . . because there never was any Christianization in the first place. Christian Europe never existed.'[5]

We confront in the historical data the same difficulties we encountered when trying to decide how to assess the strength of the Christian community today. Whether we examine affiliation, beliefs or belonging, it is difficult to reach defensible conclusions about the size and nature of the Christian community in the Christendom era. Was it ever much larger than the 10 per cent it constituted before the conversion of Constantine in the fourth century precipitated a flood of people into the imperially favoured churches? In which case, the transition from supposed majority status to contemporary minority status might be less dramatic than is claimed.

This was certainly the perspective of numerous renewal movements that disturbed the peace of Christendom in the medieval and early modern periods. Unconvinced that their society was truly Christian or that their neighbours' faith was more than skin-deep, movements such as the Hussites, Lollards, Humiliati, Waldensians, Franciscans and Anabaptists recovered a missionary stance that had long been regarded as obsolete, preached repentance, modelled and advocated a life of radical discipleship and, much to the consternation of the authorities, dared to form alternative Christian communities, sometimes even rebaptizing those who had already been baptized into a Christian society.[6] When they grew in numbers to the point at which they might be said to represent a vast minority, persecution ensured that they did not pose an even greater threat.

This perspective is shared by those today who interpret the Christendom era as a tragic and damaging deviation from the path that the

---

[4] Reports and assessments by a range of historians are collected in Rodney Stark, *The Triumph of Christianity* (New York: HarperOne, 2011), pp. 255–72.

[5] Andrew Greeley, *Religion as Poetry* (New Brunswick: Transaction Publishers, 1995), p. 63.

[6] The term 'anabaptist' means 'rebaptizer'. Anabaptists themselves, however, disowned this label and argued that infant baptism was biblically unwarranted and that they were baptizing, not rebaptizing.

Christian community should have trod. Most are rightly reluctant to recognize as true Christians only those who belonged to such movements, acknowledging that there were true Christians also within the mainstream churches. But they are also reluctant to confuse true Christianity with what they regard as 'nominal' or 'cultural' Christianity. From this perspective, nothing much has changed in recent years. The Christian community remains a vast minority.

And yet, something has changed. Even if the Christian community, measured in relation to its beliefs, practices and church attendance, was a relatively small minority throughout this era, its influence on European culture was pervasive. Latourette concludes that this minority was sufficient to 'give a tone to the Christian community'.[7] The biblical story, the authority of the church, and Christian terminology and concepts were imbibed through liturgy, art, sculpture, music, literature, architecture, legislation, customs and language. Lesslie Newbigin, reflecting on the European context after many years in India, suggested that 'Christianity had become almost the folk religion of Western Europe'.[8] Most people believed in Christendom itself as a Christian civilization that provided a framework for social, political, economic, military and cultural life. Minorities, especially vast minorities, can exercise huge influence on society, particularly if that society is unable to draw on any other philosophy or meta-narrative that is more persuasive than that to which the minority testifies.

Today, however, the influence of the Christian minority is waning. The story it tells and the beliefs that flow from this story are convincing to far fewer people. Inconsistencies between the beliefs and practices of members of the Christian community, especially its leaders, are ruthlessly exposed and discourage others from engaging with this community. Its record as a presumed majority in the Christendom era – enforcing beliefs, policing morality, engaging in violence, protecting its own status and crushing dissent – is also regarded with outrage or at least distaste. If this is to change, we must explore ways of dealing humbly and honestly with this legacy and with ongoing issues that mar the witness of the Christian community.

---

[7] Latourette, *The First Five Centuries*, p. 167.

[8] See Paul Weston, ed., *Lesslie Newbigin, Missionary Theologian: A Reader* (Grand Rapids: Eerdmans, 2006), p. 115.

But this very mixed legacy is a legacy of the church as a majority community. Whether or not we conclude that the 'true' Christian community was only ever a minority, this is not how the church perceived itself through the centuries in Europe, nor is it how the church in that era is perceived by most people today. There has been a marked, albeit gradual, transition from a widely acknowledged 'Christian culture' to a culture that recognizes that it has a 'Christian heritage'. There are aspects of this heritage that many value, even if they do not personally embrace Christian faith, and there are vestiges of this heritage scattered across our society, but few would now describe Britain unreservedly as a Christian country or contemporary culture as 'Christian'. Something has changed.

And most members of the Christian community today also recognize this change, however they assess the Christendom era and whatever continuing influence they believe or hope its heritage has. Francis Spufford describes this change very helpfully: 'The world I know, as a Christian, is the one in which we're a small minority. A small minority with an organic link to the symbolism, the buried logic and the dream-life of the wider culture, but still a minority without clout.'[9] Or, as David Voas puts it, 'the world our great-grandparents inherited was Christian in a way the one we inhabit is not.'[10]

But perceptions of this changed status are not uniform. Those who have been members of the Christian community for several decades may have personal memories of a different culture, in which the community was much larger and still had 'clout'. Congregations may never have been quite as large as they think they remember and the church's cultural and moral influence was already waning, but they rightly perceive that society has changed and the status of the Christian community is now very different. Younger members of the Christian community in most parts of Britain, on the other hand, have no personal memories of anything resembling majority status. Their experience has always been of a minority community and this has been a formative aspect of their identity as Christians. If they have any knowledge of the history

---

[9] Francis Spufford, *Unapologetic* (London: Faber & Faber, 2012), p. 220.

[10] David Voas, 'Is Britain a Christian Country?' in *Public Faith?* (ed. Paul Avis; London: SPCK, 2003), p. 92.

of their community, they will listen sympathetically to the recollections of older Christians, and the more perceptive will recognize that the Christian community has an institutional memory of majority status, even if relatively few now have personal memories of this.

Other factors also influence perceptions of the change from majority to minority status. Most inner-city churches are in contexts in which the Christian community has been a minority for many decades and in which other communities, which might be regarded as minorities in other parts of the country, are already substantially larger and more influential. In some rural areas, however, members of the Christian community may feel, rightly or wrongly, that most of their neighbours still have some allegiance towards the village church and some affinity to their beliefs and practices. Nor should we underestimate the differing perceptions in Scotland, England, Wales and Northern Ireland.

Theological perspectives and ecclesial realities also affect the way members of the Christian community experience and interpret this transition. Members of a congregation that regards itself as the local expression of a national or established church may cling on much longer to the notion of majority status than those who are members of denominations that have never aspired to such a role. Indeed, in congregations with a dissenting heritage, I frequently hear prayers of thanks for the freedom to meet together, whereas I have never heard such prayers in an Anglican church. Those who pray in this way have never personally experienced any hindrance to gathering for worship, but ingrained within the corporate memory and passed down through the generations is awareness of a minority status that is not in the communal psyche of state church members. The transition from majority to minority status within the Christian community as a whole may be less disconcerting in such communities. Members of large and growing congregations, on the other hand, especially those whose lives are lived primarily within the bubble of the Christian community, may not realize how atypical their experience is and how alien to most of those they work with or live alongside. Their eventual recognition of minority status may be theologically and emotionally very disturbing. Those who subscribe to a 'holy remnant' view of the church may conclude that the transition from majority to minority status represents a necessary pruning, whereas those whose hope is in a revived and restored Christendom may resist all talk of marginality and minority status as faithless defeatism.

These perceptions are not surprising, although they do complicate the responses the Christian community might make to its changed status. Before we consider these responses, however, we need to investigate the status, perceptions and experiences of other communities in a culture still emerging from its Christian-majority past.

Other Minorities

Undoubtedly, the most remarkable minority community is the Jewish community. Only for a small proportion of its long history has this community enjoyed majority status – in the land of Canaan after the conquest and suppression of those already living there until they were in turn conquered by Assyrian and Babylonian armies, for a brief period under the Maccabees, and much more recently after the return to the land following the Second World War. For most of the time and in most places, the Jewish community has been a small and often mistreated minority – exploited and oppressed in Egypt before the exodus; insecure and in danger of cultural assimilation in Babylon; caught up in the power struggles of the Persian, Greek and Roman empires; demonized as Christ-killers and subject to degradation, discrimination and outright persecution throughout the Christendom era. Despite occasional periods of toleration and peace, the mistreatment of the Jewish community by the Christian majority is one of the deepest stains on the history of the church.

As we ponder our future as a minority Christian community, therefore, we might ask what we can learn from the Jewish community. How did they survive? How did they sustain their faith and identity through the centuries? How did they negotiate the transition from majority status to minority status? What positive and negative consequences has minority status had? There are some resources in the Hebrew Scriptures to help us reflect on these questions, which we will consider in this chapter, but maybe we can learn also from the experiences of the Jewish community in the centuries since then.[11] And, while we must surely be slow to judge in light of the church's appalling record when we were the overwhelming majority in Europe, what can we learn from the way the Jewish majority in Israel is treating the Palestinian minority? How might the Christian community in Britain treat minorities if we ever again achieve majority status?

Perhaps the minority community with which many people in Britain are most familiar is the Muslim community. Although this community comprises people from many different nations and backgrounds, there are religious and cultural markers that distinguish it from all others. It is certainly true that theological, political and ideological diversity means that it is unfair and unwise to regard it as an undifferentiated community. It is also true that there are nominal and largely non-practising Muslims as well as deeply religious and observant Muslims.[12] But there is little doubt that information about the size of the Muslim community obtained from responses to the 2001 and 2011 census questions about religious affiliation is more accurate than that obtained about the size of the Christian community.

The Muslim community has, of course, never been a majority community in Britain, but it is an overwhelming majority in a number of other nations, as it has been for many centuries in some of these nations. The very limited toleration of minorities in these countries and active persecution of Christian, Hindu and other minorities in some of them provoke consternation in the Christian community in Britain and stimulate efforts to support and gain protection for Christians in these places. These are legitimate concerns, especially if extended to support for all minorities, not just Christians, and are shared by secular Western governments, although most are reluctant to speak out too strongly on this issue for fear of antagonizing the minority Muslim community in their own nations. But the Christian community should not ignore the

---

[11] We will return to this in a later chapter.

[12] Peter Brierley interprets 'active Muslims' as those who attend mosques at least once a year and estimates the number of these as being about 1.24 million in 2015, roughly a quarter of those identifying as Muslims. See Peter Brierley, *Pulling out of the Nosedive* (London: Christian Research, 2006), p. 4. Data from other sources indicates a similar situation in other Western nations: see *Vista* (July 2010), p. 2.

legacy of the Christendom era, in which Muslim minority communities in Europe were often discriminated against and abused. Religious majority communities, it seems, find it difficult not to persecute minorities.

Unlike the Christian community in Britain, which is currently declining, the Muslim minority community is growing. Immigration is a less significant factor now, but a higher birth rate within the Muslim community and the ability of Muslim families to retain the allegiance of a high proportion of their children mean that the percentage of the population identifying as Muslim is steadily growing. Nor should we discount the number of Westerners converting to Islam, many of these women marrying Muslim men but others attracted by the theology, morality or community life of the Muslim community. In some parts of inner-city London the Muslim community has been a majority for many years. In the early 1980s, the Anglican rector in one of these neighbourhoods received an irate telephone call insisting he stopped ringing the church bells in a Muslim area. And in several other British cities, according to the results of the 2011 census, more children are being raised as Muslims than as Christians, and the Muslim population is already or very soon will be in the majority.

The growing Muslim community is regarded with a mixture of disquiet, fear and antipathy by many in Britain, including many within the Christian community. Although these reactions are exacerbated by terrorist incidents, reports of the activities of Islamist movements in other nations and the rhetoric of extremist preachers, wariness of 'the other' appears to be at the root of these responses. It is in this context that defensive-sounding claims can still be heard that Britain is a 'Christian country'. Other unhelpful responses include conflating all Muslims together in our thinking or conversations, attempting to restrict the community's freedom to worship, educate their children or engage in missionary activities, pretending that there are no significant differences between Christianity and Islam, and expressing surprise or outrage that Muslims should want Britain to embrace Islamic values and practices.

We will explore in a later chapter more helpful and hopeful ways in which the Christian and Muslim communities might interact, but some questions are pertinent here. As we asked with reference to the Jewish community, what might we learn from the ways in which Muslims, as a minority in Britain, have sustained their community? But, unlike the Jewish community, Muslims are usually the majority in society, so how have Muslims adapted to the unfamiliar context of comprising a minority community? What can we learn from their experience as the Christian community adjusts from majority to minority status?

However we interpret the 2011 census in relation to the size of the Christian community, it is clear that other faith communities are currently much smaller. The Jewish community makes up only 0.5 per cent of the population. Sikhs comprise 0.8 per cent and Hindus 1.5 per cent. In spite of public perceptions to the contrary, the Muslim community amounts to 4.8 per cent of the population – approximately 2.7 million people. Although this community has grown by 2 per cent in the past decade, it is still substantially smaller than our best estimate of the size of the Christian community. The Christian community may now be a minority, but it remains by some distance the largest religious minority, although projections into the future suggest that this may not persist indefinitely.

There are, of course, many other smaller religious minority communities in Britain, but we should turn our attention to another community we might assume to be a sizeable majority but which actually comprises another minority – secularists. Despite the pervasive influence of secularism in schools, universities, the media and other society-shaping institutions, only 25 per cent of the population ticked 'no religion' in the 2011 census. This means just over fourteen million people and represents a 10 per cent increase since 2001 – a vast minority, confirming perceptions that British society is becoming increasingly secular, but still a minority. Some of the 7 per cent who ignored this question might, or might not, be secularists. And we might wonder if others who declared themselves to be Christians are, in fact, secularists in all but name. Other surveys of what people believe indicate that this is highly likely. But at present most people do not identify themselves as atheists, secularists, humanists (overlapping but not identical terms) or as having no religion.

While the increase in this minority community since 2001 can be interpreted as impressive or even spectacular, for advocates of the so-called 'secularization thesis' it is disappointing and even disturbing. Their confident predictions in the 1960s and 1970s of the imminent demise of religion in Europe no longer sound so convincing today. Christian communities have not disappeared, the Muslim community is growing, and other expressions of spirituality appear to be flourishing, at least in some sectors of the population. Some advocates of secularization insist that the trajectory is unaltered, even if the timescale needs to be extended; others have had second thoughts. Secularism may now be a vast minority, but it has not yet achieved the anticipated majority status. Indeed, in many Western inner-city communities, religious people significantly outnumber secularists. And recent research suggests that relatively few people, perhaps only 9 per cent of those who self-identify as 'non-religious', are consistently atheistic or secularist. The Theos think-tank, which commissioned this research, comments: 'If it is increasingly hard to sustain the claim that Britain is still a Christian country, it is even harder to claim it is an atheistic or secular one.'[13]

It is important that members of the Christian community understand this and appreciate the implications for those who are committed to a secular viewpoint. Roger Mitchell notes that 'while Christians perceive themselves to have been on the back foot, pushed increasingly towards the margins . . . the typical secular humanist feels the same way. They feel that it is the Christians who have dominated and they who have been disadvantaged.'[14] Both respond, he suggests, by becoming defensive and asserting either their ancient privileges or their more recent hard-won freedoms.

Perhaps this explains a change in the rhetoric during the past decade. Previously secularists seemed to assume religion and spirituality were waning and needed little help towards their ultimate demise. The tone among many today, especially in some sections of the media, is more belligerent and hostile. Celebrity atheists debunk religion – and especially Christianity because

[13] See http://www.theosthinktank.co.uk/comment/2012/12/12/2011-census-the-religion-question.

[14] Roger Mitchell, *The Fall of the Church* (Eugene, OR: Wipf & Stock, 2013), p. 1.

of its status in Britain as an ex-majority community.[15] Poster
campaigns encourage people to embrace life without reference to
God. Journalists gleefully expose shortcomings in the Christian
community, particularly its leaders, pour scorn on its convictions
and frequently fail to acknowledge the explicit Christian foundation and motivation of initiatives on which they otherwise report
with approval. A recent documentary on three Christian organizations in my home city of Bristol lauded their activities and their
social impact but airbrushed out all references to the Christian
faith that inspired them. Criticism of other religious communities
is more muted, whether from fear of provoking violent reactions
or from sensitivity to those who have never been more than small
minorities in Britain.

But not all secularists or atheists adopt this tone. Many realize
that atheism needs to present itself differently, explaining its positive convictions and emphasizing its contributions to human flourishing, rather than simply being anti-religious. A number of books
published in recent years have taken up this challenge.[16] The British
Humanist Association has for many years offered a much less
belligerent and more attractive alternative, distancing itself from
certain expressions of atheism. And then, during 2013, news began
to emerge of the Sunday Assembly.[17] Defining itself as 'a godless
congregation', what began as a single gathering in London is
becoming an international movement. Patterned on the activities of
the Christian community, adopting and adapting church language,
the Sunday Assembly presents itself as inclusive, non-creedal,

---

[15] Perhaps the best-known examples are Richard Dawkins. *The God
Delusion* (London: Black Swan, 2007); and Christopher Hitchens, *God
is not Great: How Religion Poisons Everything* (London: Atlantic, 2007).

[16] For example, Andre Comte-Sponville, *The Book of Atheist Spirituality*
(London: Bantam, 2009); and Chris Stedman, *Faitheist: How an Atheist
Found Common Ground with the Religious* (Boston: Beacon Press,
2013). For a helpful historical overview of atheism, see Nick Spencer,
Atheists: The Origin of the Species (London: Bloomsbury, 2014). For a
provocative exploration of historical and contemporary expressions
of atheism, see Simon Perry, *Atheism after Christendom* (Milton Keynes:
Paternoster, 2015).

[17] See http://www.sundayassembly.com. All quotations are from this
website.

celebratory and committed to making the world a better place. Its motto is 'live better, help often, wonder more', and it promises that its gatherings will 'solace worries, provoke kindness and inject a touch of transcendence into the everyday'.

Although often referred to as an 'atheist church' – and subsequently criticized for not being atheist enough by its more fundamentalist wing! – it might be more accurately described as 'secular humanist', despite the intriguing reference to 'transcendence', or even as 'secular religious'. For many years we have been familiar with the notion of people being 'spiritual but not religious' (SBNR is apparently a category on some online dating sites), but this may indicate the need for another category – 'religious but not spiritual'. It may also provoke us to question whether many 'fresh expressions of church' are missing the point by changing their format rather than their ethos. It seems that some familiar, and maybe undervalued, features of congregations – hospitality, inspirational talks, community, opportunities to engage in good works and singing uplifting songs – are appealing to those who are uninterested in the spiritual dimension of religion.[18] In a similar vein, atheist philosopher Alain de Botton notes several features of religious communities that atheists can emulate.[19]

These different strategies – belligerence, finding fault with others, presenting arguments for belief and borrowing practices from the majority community (or what was the majority) – are examples of how minority communities can commend themselves, differentiate themselves from others, respond to setbacks and seize opportunities within a changing culture. Might the Christian community, as it explores ways of flourishing as a minority community, learn from – and even in conversation with – other minority communities? Might there be helpful two-way traffic of ideas and experiences? The Sunday Assembly has learned from the churches: can the churches learn from the Sunday Assembly? The Jewish community is developing its own version of the 'fresh expressions' movement. What might the churches learn from the practices of the synagogues? And how is the Muslim community responding to the influence of secularization, especially on

---

[18] There's an interesting article on this theme at http://www.bbc.co.uk/news/magazine-27554640.

[19] Alain de Botton, *Religion for Atheists* (New York: Ransom House, 2012).

younger members of the community? Might there be things we can learn together in this shared context?

Baptist theologian Nigel Wright commends this approach:

> Other faith traditions can offer us models of what mode of existence to adopt in a world where the prevailing ideology is not our own. In particular the Jewish communities offer both positive and negative examples of how to be faithful to a calling in other environments controlled by others and how to contribute constructively to that environment . . . In many western societies it is clear enough that Muslim communities know more about nurturing and sustaining a clear community identity that even Christians do, and more about preserving the boundaries between their own community and the wider society.[20]

Advocating such mutual learning does not imply that these minority communities agree on everything or that their distinctive beliefs and practices are unimportant. It simply means that our shared experience of being minority communities might offer all of us resources – and in the process break down barriers, build relationships and increase mutual understanding. For those who are still unsure about this, there are biblical examples of the people of God in both Testaments learning from others.[21]

Is there a Majority?

Secularists have been included in this brief survey of some minority communities in Britain, despite the influence of secularism in some quarters and claims that our culture is becoming increasingly secularized. Not all will agree that secularists comprise a minority, just as others may be reluctant to abandon the notion of an enduring Christian majority. But the results of the 2011 census, when interpreted carefully and cross-referenced with other surveys, do not provide convincing evidence that either the Christian community or secularists should be accorded majority status.

---

[20] Nigel Wright, *New Baptists, New Agenda* (Carlisle: Paternoster, 2002), p. 108.

[21] For example, Jethro in Exod. 18 and Cornelius in Acts 10.

In fact, the census indicates that there is no majority community at present. British society, it seems, consists of numerous minorities, none of which currently has sufficient influence or size to be accorded majority status. Post-modern commentators suggest that our culture is a kaleidoscope of many fragments and that there is no stable pattern nor any discernible centre. Even if we are not persuaded by this analysis, which runs the risk of obscuring economic and social power dynamics, we appear to be in an era when the former majority community has lost this status but no viable successor has yet emerged.

If this is the situation, the question arises: For how long can society cohere without a new majority community emerging? Are the institutions and cultural norms established by the former majority community continuing to hold society together even though its beliefs and values are no longer espoused by most members of this society? Jeff Fountain, director of the Schuman Centre for European Studies, writes: 'Post-Christian Europeans today are squatters, living in a house without paying the rent. Our European society is a house built on a Christian legacy of values and concepts with a post-modern concoction of superstructures.'[22] For how long can this go on? When might a new majority community emerge, and which of the present minorities, if any, will this be? Two of the minority communities we have considered above might regard themselves as favourites.

If the Muslim community continues to grow over the next few decades, it is conceivable that it might be in a position by the end of the century to assume majority status. Philip Jenkins, distinguished professor of history at Baylor University, is unconvinced about this: 'If we apply to Christians the loose cultural/ethnic definition used for Muslims, then Europe's Christians presently outnumber Muslims by over twenty to one, and will continue to form a substantial majority for the foreseeable future.'[23] But this definition may not be that helpful, and one projection estimates that the number of regular mosque attenders will exceed the number of churchgoers by the year 2035.[24] More substantial

---

[22] In *Vista* 14 (2013), p. 3.

[23] Philip Jenkins, *God's Continent* (Oxford: Oxford University Press, 2007), p. 19.

[24] Reported in the 2009 edition of *Religious Trends* (Christian Research).

growth will be needed if the Muslim community is to become the majority community, but this might be a symbolically important milestone. Can Islam win the hearts of British people and offer a persuasive alternative metanarrative as a foundation for British society? Will secularism fail to provide such a foundation, and might people turn to Islam rather than turning back to Christianity?

Alternatively, the process of secularization may continue, albeit more slowly than advocates expected or wanted. In this scenario, the Christian community and other faith communities may persist indefinitely, but they will represent small minorities and have little influence on society. Muslim families might have more children than secularists, but many of these children will be secularized in due course. Fundamentalist atheism might not be attractive enough to win the allegiance of a majority, but the philosophy represented by the Sunday Assembly might have more success. Given the percentage increase of those opting for 'no religion' since the previous census, it may well be that by the time of the next census secularists will be considerably closer to attaining majority status. And yet, the term 'post-secular' is becoming increasingly common among social commentators, implying that a secular future for British society is by no means certain.[25]

Hopefully, by now, many readers will be objecting that this entire discussion appears to be ignoring the global dimension. What happens in Britain and the rest of Europe will be deeply influenced by what happens elsewhere in the world. Will the influence of secularism spread and counteract the growth of Christianity and other religions elsewhere in the world, or will the exceptionality of European secularism[26] be exposed and diminished? Will Christian or Muslim missionaries from other nations find ways of commending their beliefs to secular British people? Might this result in the Muslim community attaining majority status, or is it conceivable that the Christian community might be restored to its former majority status as British people turn away from other

---

[25] Charles Taylor, *A Secular Age* (Cambridge, MA: Harvard University Press, 2007), is a monumental study of the history, features and prospects of secularism.

[26] See Grace Davie, *Europe: The Exceptional Case* (London: Darton, Longman & Todd, 2002).

options and reappraise and rehabilitate their Christian heritage? Or might some eclectic form of spirituality pervade an otherwise secular society?

The above scenarios are, of course, merely conjectures. We cannot at this point know which, if any, of them are more likely than the others. Nor can we foresee the impact of political and economic developments, exacerbating environmental crises, shifting cultural influences and changes in the global centre of gravity as the pre-eminence of the West fades. The future of British society might involve something very different from a Muslim, secularist or Christian majority. And, as God's Spirit blows in ways we cannot predict, who knows what God has in store for us in the decades ahead?

But it is probably safe to assume that the Christian community in Britain will be a minority for the foreseeable future – a vast minority among other minorities of varying sizes – but a minority that can no longer operate as if it were a majority. Adjusting to this reality will be challenging and will not be achieved overnight. As suggested above, if we are willing, we may be able to learn much from, and alongside, other minority communities. And there are also resources in our Scriptures that might help us.

Instructions for minorities

The whole of the New Testament was written by and to members of a minority community. This is explicit in 1 Peter, the writer of which addresses his readers as 'aliens' and 'exiles', but implicit in other books. Scattered across the Roman Empire and spreading slowly eastwards beyond the boundary of that empire, Christian communities were taking root, initially in the cities and then in smaller towns and rural communities. But these were mostly quite small and nowhere did they make up more than a tiny minority of the population. They identified readily with familiar New Testament images of the Christian community as a little flock, a colony of heaven, the first fruits of the harvest and a pilgrim people.

This is the background to every book in the New Testament. Although this may sound obvious, its significance is not always appreciated. The New Testament has for centuries in Europe been read in the context of Christendom, in which the Christian community was a dominant majority. No wonder its interpretation has at times seemed forced and its radical teachings have often been muted so as not to disturb a status quo assumed to be Christian. But reading the New Testament from the perspective of a minority community frequently results in very different interpretations, as liberation theologians, Anabaptists and others have demonstrated.[27]

But the New Testament was not written to an ex-majority community. Although we may find fresh insights in these Scriptures now that we share the minority status of these early Christian communities, and although we may be able to explore different interpretations than those we have inherited from the Christendom era, there is no explicit guidance to be found on how to transition from majority to minority status. For this we must look elsewhere.

Much of the Old Testament features the people of Israel as a majority community in their own land and as a theocratic society governed by kings and priests. Their origins, however, were in an extended family of nomadic herders who comprised a tiny minority in the land of Canaan and then a growing minority in Egypt that became very threatening to the Egyptians and resulted first in escalating oppression and then the minority's flight into the desert. The subsequent conquest of Canaan and gradual expulsion or suppression of other communities transformed Israel into a nation with its own territory, in which it was the dominant majority. After a tumultuous period of conflict with surrounding nations and leadership by a series of 'judges', Israel decided to adopt the system of kingship practised by other nearby societies.

Although there is considerable ambivalence in the Old Testament as to whether kingship was a positive development,[28] it was to this sacral society that church leaders turned for guidance in the fourth and fifth centuries when the church was transitioning from minority to majority status and assuming political and social responsibilities within what was quickly becoming an officially

---

[27] See, for example, Ernesto Cardenal, *The Gospel of Solentiname* (Maryknoll: Orbis, 2010); and Lloyd Pietersen, *Reading the Bible after Christendom* (Milton Keynes: Paternoster, 2011).

[28] See, especially, 1 Sam. 8.

Christian empire. Unlike the New Testament, this section of the Old Testament had resources on which they could draw in what seemed a roughly analogous context. Subsequent history would reveal how far this approach led the church away from authentically Christian values and practices, not least in relation to issues of economics and violence. It would also demonstrate how little attention was paid to Old Testament teaching on the just treatment of minority communities by the majority. As Catholic theologian Gerhard Lohfink comments, political theology was 'enraptured with David and Solomon'. Although 'a careful look at the people of God in the Old Testament, their experiment with the state and the collapse of the experiment could have preserved the Church from repeating the old mistake', it chose to embark on 'a grandiose attempt to create a Christian empire'.[29] As the church transitions from a majority community to a minority community in Western societies, our interpretation and application of the Old Testament is one of many areas that require fresh attention.

However, there is another section of the Old Testament that has more relevance to a minority community that was previously a majority. As many have recognized, including the Swiss Reformed theologian Karl Barth as long ago as 1959,[30] there are resonances between the situation of the church in many contemporary societies and the experience of the Jews in exile in Babylon in the sixth century BCE. The imagery and language of exile is becoming very familiar as a way of describing the contemporary context, the challenges this presents and the opportunities it offers. The analogy is not, of course, perfect and we must be careful in making applications from one historical and cultural context to another, but the exilic literature is a poignant and potent scriptural resource for an ex-majority minority. Influential Old Testament scholar and preacher Walter Brueggemann has written extensively on this theme and inspired others to do so. He suggests, 'If we are indeed in exile in an alien culture, then we would do well to live inthe presence of the great exilic texts that our mothers and fathers

[29] Gerhard Lohfink, *Does God Need the Church? Toward a Theology of the People of God* (Minnesota: Liturgical Press, 1999), pp. 217–18.

[30] Karl Barth, 'Letter to a Pastor in the German Democratic Republic', in *How to Serve God in a Marxist Land* (Karl Barth and Johannes Hamel; New York: Association Press, 1959), p. 71.

formed in the exile. If we learn to trust these texts, we will have important resources to rely on.'[31]

The Jewish exiles in Babylon were struggling to come to terms with no longer being in their own land, no longer having a temple in which to worship, no longer being in charge of their own destiny. Their disorientation, grief, anger and resentment are powerfully expressed in Psalm 137, one of the most terrible biblical texts, as they yearn for their lost homeland and call down curses on the Babylonians who had devastated Jerusalem and on the Edomites who had rejoiced over their misfortunes. The short prophecy of Obadiah also castigates Edom for gloating over the city's ruin, and the prophet Habakkuk struggles to understand how God can be using the Babylonians to chastise Judah when they are more wicked and violent than even the worst of his fellow citizens. The book of Lamentations, traditionally ascribed to Jeremiah, is, as the title suggests, an extended lament over this situation.

While reactions in the Christian community to the loss of majority status and influence may not (and certainly should not) be as extreme as those exhibited by the exiles in Babylon, the exilic literature might offer resources for reflection on this situation and language for lament. Despite the ambiguities and compromises of the Christendom era, there are losses to grieve and missed opportunities to mourn. Some are also looking for others to blame for the demise of Christendom and the growing influence of secularism and other faith communities, or are hurt and offended by the way Christians are portrayed by the media. In many congregations disorientation, resentment and feelings of bereavement need to be openly acknowledged and carefully processed before the challenges and new opportunities of minority status can be explored. Brueggemann writes: 'The recovery of laments in pastoral care is a way to value the imagination of marginality, to serve the interests

---

[31] Walter Brueggemann, *Interpretation and Obedience* (Minneapolis: Fortress Press, 1991), p. 206. Examples of this include other books by Brueggemann, especially *Cadences of Home: Preaching among Exiles* (Louisville: Westminster John Knox, 1997); and more recently, Michael Frost, *Exiles: Living Missionally in a Post-Christian Culture* (Peabody: Hendricksen, 2006); and Peter McDowell, *At Home in Exile* (Belfast: Contemporary Christianity, 2012).

of social transformation, and to bear witness to a theology of the cross.'[32] But many congregations are unfamiliar with the practice of lament and have few, if any, liturgical resources. Maybe the exilic literature can be adapted or might inspire contemporary liturgists to develop their own resources.

Exile in Babylon was, however, not just distressing but an expression of divine judgement after the increasingly passionate warnings of many prophets had been ignored. If this period and its literature are to function as an analogy for the church in Western societies today, this dimension needs to be considered. How do we interpret our loss of majority status? Could this be God's judgement on our collusion with imperial values and the compromises of the Christendom era? Or should we receive it as God's gracious liberation and an opportunity to explore more authentically Christian ways of participating in society? In either case (perhaps both perspectives are needed), we might find helpful resources in the writings of Jeremiah.

Jeremiah was in no doubt that the exile represented divine judgement on unfaithful Judah, much as he lamented the destruction he had predicted. In a remarkable letter occupying much of Jeremiah 29, he warned the exiles against believing the false prophets and hoping for a quick return to Jerusalem; instead, he urged them to settle down in Babylon and learn to live faithfully in this new context. They were to resist the strong temptation to despair and invest in their future by building houses, planting crops and arranging marriages for their sons and daughters. They might now be a minority in an alien environment, but they could thrive there and increase in number.

Furthermore, rather than harbouring resentment and desires for vengeance, they were instead to 'seek the welfare of the city where I have sent you into exile' (Jer. 29:7). There were two incentives for this remarkable change of attitude. First, the Lord twice tells the exiles that he had sent them into exile (cf. v. 4) – whatever role Nebuchadnezzar and his army had played, there was divine strategy behind it. The exiles were to trust that God's good purposes would be worked out in this situation. Second, their fortunes were now intertwined with those of Babylon: if it prospered, so would they (v. 7).

---

[32] Brueggemann, *Interpretation and Obedience*, p. 194.

Perhaps this letter from Jeremiah offers perspectives that are helpful to the minority Christian community in Western societies. We need not despair – God's purposes are being worked out in ways we cannot yet fully understand. Nor need we be passive – we can invest in the future and find ways to build healthy and thriving communities. Minority status need not mean slow and steady decline – we can stabilize our numbers and even begin to grow again. But this is a time for sowing and planting rather than expectations of a bumper harvest.

There might be clues here also about how we should engage with our society. As a majority community we fell into the trap of dominating and dictating, pontificating and moralizing, and treating minorities badly. As an ex-majority community that has not experienced physical dislocation like the Jews in Babylon, we might be tempted to try to cling on to our past status and impose our will on a society we no longer control. But once we accept the futility of this and acknowledge our minority status, we could turn inwards, criticize from the sidelines and renounce any responsibility for the rest of society. Jeremiah's letter might encourage us rather to pray for (not against) our society and seek its welfare.[33]

But how do we adopt such an attitude towards a society in which we are in a minority without compromising our faith? One of the best-known sections of the exilic literature – the book of Daniel – addresses this conundrum. Leaving aside questions about the date and historicity of the book, we are presented with the story of four young Jews and their interactions with the political and religious authorities in Babylon. One of them, the eponymous Daniel, will rise to prominence, outlive the Babylonian Empire and exercise influence in the Persian Empire that succeeds it. The four do not adopt a strategy of withdrawal and non-engagement. There are cultural and religious demands to which they refuse to accede, and they accept the likelihood of suffering the consequences for such refusals, but their conversations with various officials are measured and respectful. Wherever they can, they cooperate and 'seek the welfare of the city'. Divine approval is evident in various timely interventions.

---

[33] We will return to Jer. 29 again and again in later chapters. It appears to be a biblical text that many today are consulting for guidance.

The book of Esther, set in the Persian Empire, introduces two further examples of courageous and creative engagement by members of a minority community in exile – Esther herself and Mordecai. The insecurity of the community and the threat of persecution (even genocide) are even more apparent here than in the book of Daniel, but the author commends the same motif of uncompromising engagement, rather than compromise or withdrawal, and gives further, if oblique, testimony to the gracious activity of the God who is not mentioned in the book.

Daniel and his three friends, Mordecai and Esther are examples of faithful witness and social engagement by members of an ex-majority community. Although, as with our appropriation of the exilic literature in general, we must be wary of eliding the differences between their contexts and ours, there are helpful resources here as we reflect on the tasks and possibilities of the minority Christian community in Britain and other Western societies.[34]

Finally, lest we find the laments and limited expectations of the exilic literature discouraging, it is worth noting that the exile in Babylon was profoundly significant for the Jews. This was a period of huge theological creativity as the exiles wrestled with the questions thrown up by their new context. What was God doing? What did the future hold? How did exile relate to God's promises to their ancestors? What did God require of them? What did it mean to be faithful to God in Babylon? How could they sing the Lord's song in a strange land (Ps. 137:4)? How could they worship without the Jerusalem temple? Ezekiel's prophecies and visions explore some of these questions and hold out hope of restoration and renewal.

It was in this context that the Hebrew Scriptures (our Old Testament) emerged as the exiles drew deeply on their history and heritage to make sense of their present situation. Many scholars believe that synagogues also emerged in this period, offering a

[34] It is beyond the scope of this chapter to explore the 'restoration literature' of Ezra, Nehemiah, Haggai, Zechariah and Malachi or to comment on what 'return from exile' might mean today. But the popularity of the theme of 'restoration' and its appropriation by some parts of the church in recent decades as a description of what God is doing in the church in Western societies seems premature if not misguided.

fresh expression of worship and community that would be influential in the way the early churches developed. And after centuries of vacillating between faithfulness to the Lord and idolatry, Jews in the exile finally renounced other gods and committed themselves unreservedly to the God they had discovered was with them in Babylon as well as in Jerusalem and was so much bigger than they had realized. The later chapters of Isaiah bear witness to this and to the hope that emerged from this period of something much greater than Israel's restoration.

We have the benefit of hindsight as we look back on the achievements and discoveries of the Jewish exiles in Babylon. We cannot yet tell what discoveries and achievements might result from our contemporary 'exile' (if this is how we should interpret our situation). But minority status and interaction with other communities in a plural society might stimulate theological reflection and fresh perspectives on a range of issues. We might renounce compromises that we have tolerated and justified for centuries. We might find new and more authentic ways of engaging in mission and nurturing disciples in our Christian communities. Minority or exilic status need not be resisted or accepted with resignation: we could embrace this as the way in which God is leading us at this time and be open to the challenges and opportunities ahead.

3.

Adjusting and Embracing

Although the exilic literature is especially poignant and instructive for an ex-majority community, there are other biblical passages that also resonate with our context and offer further resources for reflection. One of these occurs much earlier in the Old Testament:

> Saul clothed David with his armour; he put a bronze helmet on his head and clothed him with a coat of mail. David strapped Saul's sword over the armour, and he tried in vain to walk, for he was not used to them. Then David said to Saul, 'I cannot walk with these; for I am not used to them.' So David removed them. Then he took his staff in his hand, and chose five smooth stones from the wadi, and put them in his shepherd's bag, in the pouch; his sling was in his hand, and he drew near to the Philistine. (1 Sam. 17:38–40)

The relationship between Saul and David, the first two Israelite kings, was complex. As the narrative unfolds, Saul's attitude towards his young successor oscillates wildly between great affection and deep suspicion and antipathy. But in this early incident there is nothing to imply that Saul's gift of his armour to David was anything other than a gesture of goodwill and an attempt to protect him from the weapons of his adversary, Goliath. Like everyone else, not least Goliath, Saul assumed David was volunteering for the traditional close-quarters combat between chosen champions.

David tried on the armour but found it restrictive and debilitating. Rather than protecting him, the armour would incapacitate him, so he removed it and instead armed himself with a staff, sling and stones. The rest of the story is well known. Goliath was offended when he saw how young and poorly armed David was, but David proclaimed that the God of Israel was on his side, took aim and toppled the Philistine with a shot to the forehead. Generations of children have marvelled at this heroic encounter and its apparently surprising outcome (storytellers usually omit the part where David decapitates Goliath and displays his bloody head). But the outcome was actually far from surprising: a heavily armed and cumbersome warrior had little chance against a nimble and experienced slinger. As long as David kept out of range and was accurate with his stones, Goliath was in trouble. The Lord's deliverance of Israel from their enemies on this occasion owed much to David changing the rules of engagement.[1]

What has this famous incident to do with the challenges facing the Christian community in Britain as we come to terms with being a vast minority? Without stretching the analogy too far, we might wonder whether we are as weighed down by the trappings of the past as David was by Saul's armour. That armour was no doubt very impressive. It had served Saul well and it was a generous gift to David. But it was an encumbrance that hindered rather than helped him – and it would have got him killed if he had not taken it off. Staff, stones and a sling did not look very impressive, but they were all David needed. Being light on his feet and accurate in his aim was much more important than being well protected, resplendent and heavily armed.

A minority community that used to be a majority faces difficult decisions about the legacy of its past status. The post-Christendom church is heir to wonderful treasures and rich resources. Even those who are most critical of the church's collusion with empire and its very chequered history over many centuries cannot deny that this era produced stunning achievements in many areas of human life and culture. And even those who are most deeply committed to a secular future rarely dismiss those achievements or propose that they are swept away without residue. But there is also plenty of dross that was never of much value and is certainly not worth preserving. And, between the gold and the dross, there are many aspects of this legacy that might once have been life-giving

---

[1] For an intriguing discussion of this incident and some contemporary applications, see Malcolm Gladwell, *David and Goliath: Underdogs, Misfits and the Art of Battling Giants* (London: Penguin, 2014).

and useful to the community but are now trappings that weigh us down, distract us or damage our ability to respond creatively to a changed and changing context. Transitioning to minority status will require discernment, sensitivity and courage. It will involve a thorough review of all aspects of the life of the community. What follows is a sample, a starter.

Resources

The Christian community in Britain today may be a minority but it is a vast minority with huge resources. It is a wealthy community with an enormous amount of property, some of it in prime locations and worth huge sums of money. Many of these buildings contain valuable paintings, sculptures, fabric and furniture. Despite the impact of recession on share prices, its investments are extensive and worth billions of pounds. And we have already noted that the closure and sale of buildings as a majority community adjusts to being a minority has meant that the financial resources of some declining denominations have soared. Furthermore, if the Christian community equates to roughly 10 per cent of the population, its capacity to raise funds is beyond the scope of most organizations – not least because many in this community are willing to give generously and repeatedly to causes they believe in.

Church treasurers, theological college bursars, Christian charity fundraisers and those with responsibility for denominational finances may not react very well to the previous paragraph. Many congregations, colleges and organizations are struggling to survive in the face of rising costs, diminishing donations, fewer legacies, increasing pension demands, the repair bills on buildings (often exacerbated by their listed status) and the tendency of donors to support other causes than institutional maintenance. It seems laughable to suggest that the Christian community is awash with resources. But it is!

Of course, we do not have financial resources on the scale we had when we were the majority community, nor would we expect this. But we have a remarkable legacy from that period and the ability to fund pretty much anything we want to. The question we face is what to prioritize and what to relinquish. As a vast minority with huge inherited and current resources, the issue is not whether we have sufficient but how we choose to use these resources.

The capacity of the Christian community to release resources and use these creatively was evident in Fremantle, Australia, a few years ago. In 2003 several churches in the town were challenged by the 'jubilee' vision in Leviticus 25 and decided to explore ways to practise this. Initially, they did what many churches have done – they distributed Christmas hampers to families in need. They raised AUD$40,000 and gave away 10 tons of food to 500 families. The following Easter they went further. The sixteen churches in the town raised enough money to pay off the utility bills (gas, electricity and water) of any residents threatened with having their services cut off and the rent arrears of any residents threatened with eviction. Working with the utility companies and the local housing authority, they identified those in need and donated over AUD$120,000 to release the debts of all those affected. Nobody expected this action to prevent all the beneficiaries getting into debt again, although it offered them an opportunity to make a fresh start, but it represented a glimpse of God's inbreaking kingdom and the practical application of a radical but neglected principle of biblical economics. If this is what a few churches in a small town could do, imagine what is possible for a vast minority with colossal resources![2]

No doubt some will object that the Christian community has colossal obligations too and cannot simply release its abundant resources. This is true and there are certainly hard choices to be made if these resources are to be deployed in ways that will both sustain the Christian community and enable it to engage creatively and imaginatively in God's mission. But in this period of transition from majority to minority status, these choices need to be made.

There is a huge amount of duplication and waste in the Christian community. Whatever the historical reasons and contemporary justifications for this, and however problematic it will be to challenge the vested interests involved, we need to address

---

[2] See further Kim Tan, *The Jubilee Gospel: The Jubilee, Spirit and the Church* (Milton Keynes: Authentic Media, 2008), pp. 131–2.

this scandalous situation. There are too many church buildings in most areas: if congregations would share their buildings the redundant buildings could be sold, significantly reducing costs and raising funds that can be invested in more sensible ways. There are too many theological colleges struggling to attract staff and students and to pay their way: merging would reduce over-heads and provide a much richer learning environment. There are too many Christian organizations competing for funds, as grant-making charities will tell anyone who will listen, many of them engaging in similar activities. Joining together makes financial sense and might enable more effective mission and ministry. And, as anyone working across denominations will affirm, there are too many denominations replicating each other's staff, departments, programmes and initiatives.

An ex-majority community needs to rationalize its resources, reduce waste and address the issue of duplication. A minority community does not have the luxury of kowtowing to vested interests and indulging in nostalgia. Some of the necessary steps will be complex and require skilled and persistent leadership. Some will be painful as precious places and institutions are evacu-ated. But the alternative is an economy of scarcity, anxiety and the eventual closure of buildings, institutions and organizations that a minority community can no longer afford. The wasted resources will have become wasted opportunities. Too often mergers take place only when resources are running out and, despite the rhet-oric of merging for the sake of mission, the prevailing mindset is one of desperation and survival. This usually exacerbates decline. We need to act sooner and resist the temptation to dismiss this strategy as simplistic and unrealistic. Reducing waste and dupli-cation would release substantial resources within the Christian community.

We face hard choices in other areas too. For how long do we subsidize churches, ministers and organizations that are appar-ently making little impact and how do we assess this? What proportion of our resources do we invest in experimental initia-tives that might discover fresh and effective approaches to mission and discipleship, but might equally be short-lived and impotent? How long do we support such risky initiatives? What are the risks of not investing in this way? Will suburban churches continue to fund large staff teams that deprive most of their members of the opportunity to be participants rather than passengers, or might some choose to fund pioneers, pastors and community workers in small urban churches engaged in mission and ministry in areas of multiple deprivation? When will bi-vocational ministry (or bi-ministerial ministry or omni-vocational ministry)[3] be welcomed as the norm, rather than the exception, as a missional approach to ministry rather than a regrettable necessity in cash-strapped congregations? And do we invest our very substantial resources in ways that will maximize our income or disinvest in companies with practices that damage the earth and do not promote human flourishing?

As a minority community we cannot continue to fund everything we could when we were a majority. The financial pressures many denominations, organizations and congregations are facing today will become even greater unless difficult decisions are made about what is essential and what is not. Saul's armour is weighing us down. We cannot walk around in it much longer. However beautiful and impressive it is, we need something more flexible and better suited to the challenges ahead. And our approach needs to be more imaginative and more radical than a series of funding cuts and minor adjustments.

It is not easy to hold together these two realities – serious financial shortages in many sectors of the Christian community, which continue to operate as they did when they were part of a majority community, and the abundant resources available if only we accept that we are now a minority community and need to operate in different ways. If we see only scarcity and can envisage nothing beyond less of what we have now, we will remain locked into a depressing cycle of decline. But if we are willing to think in creative ways about how a minority might use its resources differently, all kinds of new possibilities might open up. A vast minority has vast resources, but we need to deploy them wisely and not waste them on what is no longer appropriate and will soon be unsustainable.

---

[3] A neologism coined by an urban church in Manchester planted under the auspices of Urban Expression (http://www.urbanexpression.org.uk).

People

We face a similar challenge in relation to what our culture, enslaved by economic categories, insists on calling 'human resources', but which we will choose to call 'people'. The Christian community is not as numerous as we once were. Congregations all over the country plead for volunteers to help run their programmes, join committees and take responsibility for a wide range of activities. Ageing communities rely on the loyalty and sheer doggedness of members who would have retired years ago if there was anyone willing to succeed them. And younger members, for a number of reasons, shy away from taking on these responsibilities. Some who might otherwise volunteer are understandably fearful of open-ended commitments with no further successor in view. Others are reluctant because of external factors, including work pressures, both partners in a couple working in order to afford the rent or mortgage, increased commuting times that preclude midweek church activities, blended and more complicated families, and many more leisure options. And others may be wary of committing time to a declining Christian community, in which voluntary service no longer carries the social status or kudos it once did and the effort involved may do little but prolong the inexorable decline. This issue is not, of course, unique to the churches. It is affecting most organizations today that depend on regular voluntary support. The Christian community is not immune from the influence of what some term a 'post-commitment' culture.

But how many of these roles and responsibilities are really necessary? Undoubtedly, some of them are if the Christian community is to sustain its corporate life and nurture the capacity of its members to participate in God's mission in the world. But some will need to go. This will be true also of regional and national denominational roles, to which it is often harder to attract volunteers. Richard Koenig writes: 'As the de-christianization of society continues, it appears that the denomination is perhaps the hardest hit of all religious institutions.'[4] Some of these voluntary roles are vital if the community is not to become unhealthily parochial and lose its interconnectedness and ability to operate at other levels of

[4] Richard Koenig, *A Creative Minority: The Church in a New Age* (Minneapolis: Augsburg, 1971), p. 105.

society. But others may be unnecessary for a minority community, or will at least need to be reconfigured and refocused. This is true also for those in paid national or regional roles. Some may simply be redundant and others will need to transition from being 'fire-fighters' (spending much of their time dealing with institutional and relational problems) to 'arsonists' (inspiring, encouraging and nurturing creative mission initiatives).[5] Learning to operate more as a network or movement will take time and require significant adjustments in our thinking and practice, but this will release time and energy and will help the Christian community to become more nimble and flexible.

The image of David struggling in Saul's armour reappears. Many (though certainly not all) of the activities to which the Christian community has been committed were appropriate and fruitful in a previous generation, but some are now a weight we can no longer carry. Coming to terms with being a minority community requires a thorough review of what we are doing and why, whether these activities are sustainable, what they are achieving and whether we should be concentrating on doing fewer things more effectively. We may conclude that there are some things we should stop doing altogether, some that we should do less often or in different ways, and some to which we should give greater priority. Reducing activities and limiting commitments can be interpreted as defeatist and a cause for regret, but these are vital if we are to avoid burning each other out and release the energy and flexibility we need to engage creatively with a diverse and changing culture.

I have argued elsewhere that in a post-Christendom context we will need to simplify church life and apply a 'double sustainability' test: are our activities sustainable and do they sustain the community?[6] Different churches may reach different conclusions as they apply this test, but asking these questions and assessing honestly and rigorously the feedback from the community will help us adjust to being a minority community.

A process resembling this is already underway in some sections of the Christian community. Committees and working groups,

---

5 I cannot recall where I came across this compelling image.

6 Stuart Murray, *Church after Christendom* (Milton Keynes: Paternoster, 2005), pp. 217–32.

programmes and meetings, departments and activities have been disbanded and discontinued in an ecclesial equivalent of the 'bonfire of the quangos' announced by the incoming coalition government in 2010. Time will tell how effective this cull has been. Will it result in the release of energy and fresh initiatives? Or is it primarily about saving money and institutional survival? How many of these structures and activities will reappear in a different guise? Or is this evidence of a mindset shift and willingness to adjust to the realities of being a minority community? *Why* we do this is as important as what we do.

And the main purpose of this institutional and structural simplification is to release the vast minority from pressures that are becoming unbearable and into ways of living that enable the Christian community to thrive and bear faithful witness in contemporary culture. To sustain this community in a culture that offers little support for faithful discipleship and presents many challenges will require us to be much more intentional in what we do together and waste less time on activities that drain and do not truly sustain us. We will return to this in the next chapter. But reducing the internal demands of church life holds out the prospect of freeing us to participate more joyfully and energetically in the mission of God.

If the vast minority really does approximate to 10 per cent of the population, there are over six million members of the Christian community. This represents an enormous capacity to participate in the mission of God. Despite the pressures and disincentives we have mentioned, and even with overburdensome church programmes, many are already involved in a vast range of missional activities in their neighbourhoods, in their workplaces, in political activism, in business enterprises, in social movements, in caring for the environment, in working for justice, and much else.

Estimates of the economic value of this plethora of voluntary ministry reveal an extraordinary generosity in the use of time and energy. Roger Standing, for example, reports: 'In the late 1990s, a South London borough commissioned a survey of community life and provision and was staggered by how far the well-being of the borough rested on the community engagement of the churches. They concluded that the total value of this, in terms of social capital, was beyond their ability as local government ever to finance or provide.'[7] And journalist Simon Jenkins, noting that the Church of England alone manages to 'mobilise 1.6 million parish volunteers for what amounts to social work, from caring for the elderly to hospital visiting' comments: 'This output must be worth billions to the state', and complains: 'All the state does in return is impose VAT and health and safety regulations on church repairs.'[8]

The term 'social capital' has become popular as a way of describing this investment in the life and wellbeing of the wider community. Many others beyond the Christian community, of course, also invest hugely in such activities, but various studies have concluded that the proportion of the Christian community doing so is significantly higher than the proportion of the general population.[9] And the size of the Christian community, even as a minority, is such that it often dwarfs the contributions of other organizations. A statement on the Diocese of Oxford's website, for example, claims that its 'unique combination of buildings, volunteers, voluntary giving and involvement in the lives of the community makes it the largest self-funded voluntary organization in the Thames Valley',[10] And Paul Cloke, professor of human geography at Exeter University, notes that a study in Northern Ireland indicated that two-thirds of registered youth groups and three-quarters of registered youth leaders are faith-based.[11] He suggests that a majority of youth work across the UK is faith-based. And it is clear that faith is the primary motivation, so maybe the term 'spiritual capital' is at least as appropriate.

Simon Jenkins continues:

[7] Roger Standing, *As a Fire by Burning* (London: SCM Press, 2013), p. 21.

[8] Writing in *The Guardian* (21 Dec. 2012).

[9] See, for example, Paul Avis, ed., *Public Faith?* (London: SPCK, 2003), pp. 58–61. The term 'social capital' is another example of the tendency to reduce all activities to economic categories.

[10] See http://www.oxford.anglican.org.

[11] Paul Cloke, 'Faith-based Youth Work in Local Communities: The Teenbridge Project', in *Working Faith: Faith-Based Organizations and Urban Social Justice* (ed. Paul Cloke, Justin Beaumont and Andrew Williams; Milton Keynes: Paternoster, 2013), p. 113.

The church and its clergy are one of the last human threads binding villages, towns and inner city communities together . . . I have visited estates outside Sheffield, Manchester and East London from which doctors, teachers, policemen, social workers, professionals of all sorts, have fled, or at least confined themselves to cars. The only 'leader' left in residence is the priest, of whatever denomination, underpaid, working in appalling surroundings and motivated by a grim but sincere philanthropy. The nearest I have found to saints have been priests in tough areas.[12]

And philosopher Jack Caputo writes in a similar vein:

If, on any given day, you go into the worst neighbourhoods of the inner cities of most large urban centres, the people you will find there serving the poor and needy, expending their lives and considerable talents attending to the least among us, will almost certainly be religious people . . . They are down in the trenches, out on the streets, serving the widow, the orphan and the stranger, while the critics of religion are sleeping in on Sunday mornings.[13]

This tribute is quoted in a collection of essays entitled *Working Faith*, which investigates the growing role of 'faith-based organizations' in a secular and post-secular society.[14] The authors identify a range of factors, within the churches and in society, that are opening up all kinds of fresh opportunities for the Christian community, and present several case studies of effective social engagement. They recognize the danger of these initiatives being co-opted politically and of the Christian community being used to deliver social services more cheaply than the state can provide, but they advocate strongly for discerning engagement and for the capacity of faith-based organizations to make a distinctive contribution that both ministers to those in need and challenges the prevailing neoliberal ideology.[15]

[12] Cloke, 'Faith-based Youth Work', p. 113.
[13] Jack Caputo, *On Religion* (London: Routledge, 2001), p. 92. Caputo notes that Jewish and Muslim volunteers can also be found in these settings.
[14] Cloke, Beaumont and Williams, *Working Faith*.
[15] The Cinnamon Network is undertaking extensive research into the contribution of faith-based groups and plans to present its findings

Six million members of the Christian community also represent vast evangelistic potential – if we are not so ensnared by internal church programmes and responsibilities that we have few relationships outside this community, and if we discover how to share our faith authentically and sensitively in a culture that is deeply suspicious of evangelism. Research confirms that most people become followers of Jesus because they see the Christian faith lived out by someone they know and trust.[16] Such relationships will flourish if we have time and energy to invest in them, not manipulatively and with ulterior motives, but in genuine friendship.

Some members of the Christian community have sadly felt obliged to disengage from church in order to participate in the wider community, volunteer in all kinds of social projects and be able to spend time with friends and neighbours. Simplifying church and ensuring that church activities are sustaining rather than draining might release many more to be involved in these ways and might encourage those who have disengaged to reconnect and find support within the churches for their missional activities.

Expectations

Assessing the resources available to the Christian community and the size of this community, now a minority but still vast, requires us to be realistic but encourages us to be hopeful. There are things we can no longer do, things we no longer need to do, things we should never have done anyway, but also new opportunities and possibilities. We will need to choose carefully which battles to fight and what projects to take up, but we have the people and the resources to do just about anything we commit ourselves to – as long as we are prepared to strip off the equivalent of Saul's armour and walk around more freely.

[15] cont. in mid-2015. See: http://www.cinnamonnetwork.co.uk/cinnamon-faith-action-audits.

[16] Extensive evidence was provided in John Finney, *Finding Faith Today* (Swindon: Bible Society, 1996). The significance of relationships is undiminished in his more recent book, *Emerging Evangelism* (London: Darton, Longman & Todd, 2011).

What, then, might be the capacity of the Christian community? What can we hope for? What expectations are realistic? There are wildly divergent expectations within the Christian community, ranging from imminent revival to inexorable decline and marginalization. The conclusion at the end of Chapter 1 – some numerical growth is feasible but minority status will persist for the foreseeable future – may not persuade those at either end of this spectrum, but this is the basis for the following chapters. Our expectations, in any case, must not be restricted to the size of the Christian community but include other dimensions, not least its ability to interact creatively and missionally with the rest of society.

In Chapter 2 we reflected briefly on Jeremiah's letter to the exiles in Babylon. He was not uninterested in the size of the community, encouraging the exiles to increase in number rather than expecting to decrease. But the main thrust of his advice was related to the community's impact on a society they regarded as alien and hostile, because their own welfare was now inextricably linked with the welfare of their neighbours in Babylon. Our expectations, too, must include, maybe prioritize, the capacity of the Christian community to participate in and bless a society in which we are now a minority.

Perhaps we should first identify expectations that are unrealistic for a minority, however vast, and especially one widely regarded as an ex-majority with a questionable track record and little to offer a society moving away from Christian convictions and practices.

So it is unrealistic for the Christian community to expect to retain the privileges it enjoyed as a majority community. Some of these privileges have already been lost, but others remain as vestiges of a past culture. These include Christian prayers daily in both Houses of Parliament, bishops in the House of Lords, churches enjoying the presumption that their activities are charitable and so eligible for significant tax benefits, the use of oaths in the law courts, and schools required to provide daily acts of collective worship 'wholly or mainly of a broadly Christian character'.[17] Adjusting to minority status will mean choosing not to cling on

---

[17] A more extensive list can be found in Stuart Murray, *Post-Christendom* (Carlisle: Paternoster, 2004), pp. 189–93.

to these privileges or plead for special treatment but to advocate for the equitable treatment of all in a plural society. The credibility and witness of the Christian community will be enhanced if it champions the rights and interests of other communities rather than trying to defend its own interests.

It is unrealistic for the Christian community to expect its institutions, pronouncements, views and beliefs to be accorded greater respect than those of any other community. Church synods and conferences can pass motions; denominational representatives can lobby politicians; and Christians in various walks of life can contribute to public debates. These contributions may or may not be influential or effective, but they are no longer privileged over contributions from other interest groups. Statements by senior Anglican and Catholic clerics still receive a surprising amount of attention in the media, but these are scrutinized and challenged by those who hold different views. And the views of secularists and leaders of other faith groups are accorded as much respect. As a vast minority, the Christian community has opportunities and responsibilities to speak out on all kinds of issues, but it does so as a minority and should not expect, demand or hanker after special treatment.

It is unrealistic for the Christian community to expect always to be portrayed sympathetically or fairly in the media. Church members frequently complain about the characterization (or caricaturing) of Christians in television dramas, about the tendency of news programmes to feature eccentric or extremist representatives of the Christian community, and about the ways in which Jesus is portrayed in films, plays and musicals. Documentaries about the practices of some parts of the Christian community also make uncomfortable viewing, as do programmes about the historical record of the church as a majority community. There is no reason why we should not express concern about bias and misrepresentation, especially if we also express such concern when other minority communities are portrayed unfairly, but we should not be surprised or outraged by such portrayals. An ex-majority community is understandably 'fair game' for such treatment in a way that other minorities are not.

It is unrealistic for the Christian community to expect to maintain 'national coverage' with reduced personnel and resources.

Accepting this will be especially hard for denominations, such as the Church of England and the Church of Scotland, which have been committed to this through the parish system and whose sense of identity is closely connected to this notion. Sir Tony Baldry, Second Church Estates Commissioner, recently warned: 'The Church of England probably has no more than 20 years to reassert its position as the national Church of England.'[18] But is this a realistic prospect? The Church of England website carries the bold strapline 'a Christian presence in every community', but this presence is highly attenuated in many places now. And the Church of Scotland website claims that 'Church of Scotland parish churches play a crucial part across a range of communities, from remote villages to deprived urban areas where shops, banks, schools and other institutions have disappeared'.

While attempts to maintain national coverage and to serve local communities from which other institutions are disappearing are laudable, these attempts may soon place unbearable burdens on those who are expected to embody this Christian presence. National coverage might be feasible for some time yet if partnership between denominations allowed for the merging of congregations and reduced duplication of overstretched resources, but very often vested interests preclude this. A minority Christian community will need to come to terms with the reality that some parts of the country are already devoid of 'Christian presence' and more soon will be. As a vast minority, we have the resources to respond to this challenge, but this will require a missional strategy rather than pretending an obsolete system of national coverage is still in place.

It is unrealistic for the Christian community to exercise the amount of influence it once had in many areas of society, to operate on its own, or to expect to control all the organizations and initiatives in which it participates. The Christian community has an impressive track record of ministry to individuals and families in need, speaking out for the marginalized, caring for the vulnerable, creating new institutions, galvanizing local communities and raising substantial funds to support such initiatives. As austerity measures continue to penalize the poor for the misdeeds of the rich, and as the limitations of the welfare state become

18 Quoted at http://www.bbc.co.uk/news/uk-23215388.

apparent, there will be fresh opportunities for the Christian community to 'seek the welfare' of society and to take initiatives in many areas of social and cultural life as previous generations did. It is doubtful whether any other organization has a similar capacity to this vast minority. But the lessons of the past need to be learned, and the realities of the present need to be recognized. Patronizing, controlling and manipulative attitudes and practices have no place. Furthermore, rather than bemoaning the limitations of being a minority, the Christian community needs to be wary of using its clout as a vast minority to exercise influence or exert pressure in inappropriate ways.

If these expectations are unrealistic, what might we more realistically expect and commit our time, resources and energy towards?

It is difficult to know how to respond to members of the Christian community who are hoping and praying passionately for revival. It is also unclear what most imagine revival might look like today. Revivals in Western contexts during the past three or four centuries have impacted societies imbued with Christian culture and in which church attendance was normal, if not as ubiquitous as sometimes thought, and the Christian community was a majority. Revivals were periods in which consciences were pricked, faith grew, commitment was deepened, spiritual fervour increased, moral standards were lifted and, in some cases, the effects were felt across society. Some studies have identified problematic aspects of these revivals, or at least of their aftermath, although it would seem churlish to denigrate their impact. But these revivals were predicated on a very different culture from ours, so it may be unrealistic to expect something similar. It may also represent a hankering for the past or reluctance to embrace the purposes of God in the present. Jeremiah warned the exiles in Babylon to stop yearning for Jerusalem, to reject the assurances of false prophets that they would soon be going home, and to settle down in Babylon and trust in God's good purposes in this situation. Praying for revival is not helpful if we are hoping for a return to Christendom or evading the challenge of learning how to live and thrive in post-Christendom.

How, then, might we pray? What might we expect? Jeremiah encouraged the exiles to build and plant, to put down roots, physically and emotionally, and to learn to live faithfully in the present.

Perhaps, rather than expecting an abundant harvest in the near future ('revival' and 'harvest' are often linked in the literature and the language of prayers for revival), we need to recognize that there is work to be done before any harvest can be expected. Sowing precedes harvesting, and there is watering and tending to be done between sowing and harvesting. And before the sowing, hard ground often needs to be broken up. Maybe this should be the focus of our praying and our activity. As a vast minority, we have the capacity to sow generously in all kinds of contexts and to water what begins to grow, but we will need to be patient and not lose heart. There may also be hard ground to break up in our culture and in our churches, and (to change the agricultural image slightly) not a little pruning. It is not unrealistic to expect some growth in the years ahead,[19] rather than continuing decline, but a bumper harvest may be some way off.

It is unrealistic to expect a minority community to be able to impose its will on society in the way that a majority community did, but it is not unrealistic to expect a minority community with distinctive convictions and practices to have a profound influence on society if it lives out what it advocates. Minority communities throughout history have done this. However, there are particular challenges facing an ex-majority community, especially one guilty not only of imposition in the past but also of often failing to embody in practice what it proclaimed. A post-Christendom society will be understandably wary of the Christian community and very reluctant to allow it to have too much influence beyond its own constituency. It will seize on examples of immoral behaviour, intolerant attitudes, inconsistency and disunity, publicize these mercilessly, and thereby blunt any challenges the Christian community presents or any awkward questions it poses. If the Christian community is to fulfil its potential as a minority, we

[19] According to *Life in the Church?*, a research project published in June 2013 by the Evangelical Alliance, 71 per cent of evangelicals expected their own church to grow over the next twenty years (13 per cent dramatically and 58 per cent somewhat), albeit just 47 per cent currently were; but only 41 per cent expected the wider UK church to grow (against 45 per cent anticipating a decrease, 29 per cent dramatically and 16 per cent somewhat). See http://www.eauk.org/church/resources/snapshot/upload/church-life-report-may-2013.pdf.

must present a more compelling witness than we currently do. Perfection is not required, but authenticity, honesty, credibility and humility are.

Realistically, given the disunited state of the Christian community and the distrust towards the church as an institution revealed by pollsters, we are much more likely to be effective at the grass roots and in local communities than at any other level. This is the conclusion of a perceptive article by Andrew Brown, who reports[20] that 'more people under 24 believe the church is a force for bad in society than suppose it's a force for good'. He is addressing the Church of England, but his advice is relevant to all denominations: 'Instead of pretending it is a single coherent entity with clearly defined opinions and policies . . . it should just forget about the national level and get on with things locally.' He urges the General Synod to 'shut up', because nobody pays any attention unless it says something crass and repulsive, and argues that the best hope for the future lies, not in top-down posturing and pontificating, but in the unglamorous but faithful witness of local congregations. This is where credibility might be established and the Christian community can make a creative contribution to the wellbeing of society. In a culture that is suspicious of all institutions, not just the church, this makes a lot of sense, especially given the vast resources and personnel of the Christian community at a local level, but a bottom-up approach will require patience and realistic expectations.

Patience is certainly one of the virtues required of an ex-majority community with a dubious heritage struggling for credibility as a minority community. It will take time to gain the trust of a society that has rejected the Christendom version of the Christian faith. It will take time for the Christian community to disavow practices and attitudes that marred its witness in the past and are utterly inappropriate now. It will take time to learn to live as exiles in an alien culture, as a minority alongside other minorities in a plural culture. And it will be some time yet before Western societies realize the extent to which our institutions are bereft of spiritual and moral foundations, our culture has no compelling vision of the future, and post-modern relativism is inadequate for safeguarding human life and dignity. It is just possible that the search

---

[20] Andrew Brown, 'The Church Must Go Local', *The Guardian* (26 December 2013), p. 39.

for a new consensus on which to build a sustainable culture might include a fresh look at the Christian story, especially if the Christian community has learned by then to embody its convictions and values in a credible and attractive way.

Thinking and Speaking

Realistic expectations will impact the way we think and speak as a minority community. It is likely that Saul's expectations of what David might accomplish against Goliath were already low and were not heightened when David exchanged a suit of armour for a sling and stones. It is clear that Goliath expected nothing else than a quick and rather inglorious victory over the young upstart who now faced him. His attitude towards David was dismissive (1 Sam. 17:42–4). But David was seemingly unfazed by these expectations of what he might achieve, declaring his reliance on the God of Israel to bring about the right outcome (vv. 45–7). We will eschew his bloodthirsty intentions, but we might emulate his quiet confidence. An ex-majority community, aware that it has lost ground within society and that its convictions and practices are treated with widespread disdain, needs to think carefully about how it views itself, what it says and how it says it.

A minority community with memories of being a majority faces a number of temptations in the way it thinks about itself and its context. If we succumb to these temptations, it will take longer for us to adjust to our new status and damage our credibility and capacity to interact creatively with our society. Among these temptations are:

- Nostalgia: rather than facing forward, we look back to whatever period we identify as 'the good old days' (usually through rose-tinted spectacles) and retreat into a mixture of sadness, resignation and half-hearted hopes that those days might return if only we could find a way to restore whatever practices we think produced them.
- Defensiveness: an ex-majority community in a society that has largely rejected what it stands for is prone to be criticized for its past failings and its present inadequacies. It is tempting to

retreat into a beleaguered and defensive posture, rather than examining these criticisms carefully, taking on board what is justified and openly acknowledging weaknesses and areas of unfaithfulness.

- Defeatism: although we may recoil from admitting it, we may wonder if we have any kind of future, whether the gospel is no longer effective, whether there is anything we can do, and whether God has given up on us. This way of thinking saps our energy, leads to introversion, makes our community deeply unattractive and accelerates decline.

- Self-importance: if we lose heart in relation to our capacity to impact those around us, we can become self-absorbed and develop a 'holy remnant' perspective, ignoring the needs and aspirations of the rest of society, convincing ourselves that God is solely or at least primarily interested in our community, and often indulging in infighting over minutiae.

- Resentment: this may be focused on church leaders (local and translocal) for their supposed shortcomings, on other sections of society that seem to receive preferential treatment, on those who criticize or disparage the Christian community, or on anyone else who can reasonably or unreasonably be held responsible for the diminished status of the Christian community. But grumpiness is no more attractive than defeatism.

- Scaremongering: loss of privilege, disdain, criticisms, restrictions and mockery can easily result in a persecution complex – and the language of 'persecution' has become more common in the Christian community in recent years. With very few exceptions, this perception is unjustified and overblown. It provokes anxiety and also devalues the suffering of our brothers and sisters in other societies who are experiencing genuine persecution. Alternatively, this kind of scaremongering can fuel extremism and lead to xenophobia and violence in supposed defence of a 'Christian' culture. An appalling example was the massacre carried out by Norwegian Anders Brevik, who killed seventy-seven people in 2011 when he bombed central Oslo and then opened fire at an island youth camp. His defence was that he was a modern-day crusader fighting the Islamization of Europe and defending Christendom. Much less extreme but still deeply disturbing are attempts by right-wing political parties, such as the British National Party, to play on these fears and present themselves as defenders of Christendom. The Christian community would do well to avoid any such scaremongering.

Summing up his concerns about the temptations facing an ex-majority community, Richard Koenig concludes: 'It is when things do not go well that the debates break out, uncertainty manifests itself, nostalgia turns into near despair . . . The churches accordingly need to develop a new attitude, a new outlook, a new self-understanding, adequate for and expressive of their real location in society. This must be something different from a blind triumphalism, a helpless nostalgia, or suicidal accommodation.'[21]

Emulating David's quiet confidence and reliance on God (and disavowing his desire to wreak vengeance on his enemy) is challenging in this transitional period, even if we recognize that we still constitute a vast minority with remarkable resources. But this is a more sustainable foundation for the Christian community than either despair or hyped expectations.

There are temptations also in relation to how the Christian community speaks about itself and its concerns. Among these are:

- Arrogance: memories of being a respected majority community and of its spokesmen (almost always men) speaking with authority on political, economic and social issues as well as moral and spiritual matters may still in some circles encourage statements and pronouncements that now sound arrogant, pontificating and quite inappropriate for a minority community. This blustering evinces lack of confidence and may well be interpreted as the ecclesial equivalent of 'small man syndrome'!
- Monologue: closely connected to pontificating is the tendency to engage primarily in monologue rather than dialogue, to speak too quickly rather than listening attentively and reflecting carefully. Monologue preaching has been dominant in many churches for so long that the skills of dialogue are often very underdeveloped. Perhaps asking awkward and provocative questions might be more effective than offering answers – especially if these are answers to questions not being asked! After all, Jesus seems to have favoured asking questions and telling

---

[21] Koenig, *A Creative Minority*, pp. 28–30.

puzzling stories rather than answering the questions people asked him.

- Moralizing: the language of 'ought' and 'should' and efforts to reassert the status of the Christian community as some kind of moral arbiter or guardian of society are not helpful. Abandoning a 'moral majority' position in favour of a 'prophetic minority' perspective is more realistic and might be much more interesting, especially if this is combined with contrition for past failures and humility about present inadequacies.
- Special pleading: there is a difference between speaking out prophetically against injustice in society and standing up for our own rights and preferences. A minority community, especially an ex-majority community, needs to ensure it speaks out on behalf of others as well as defending its own interests.
- Belligerence: grumpiness and resentment can easily result in hostile language and a hectoring or complaining tone, as a minority community finds fault with features of a culture it no longer dominates or can hope to control.
- Silence: not all members of the Christian community will succumb to the temptations listed above. Some, confused by their change of status, cowed by opposition, disdain and criticisms, sensitive to past and present failures, will choose to withdraw and say little or nothing. In some contexts, this may be a wise choice and more effective than any words could be, but the Christian community still has a responsibility, despite our many shortcomings, to tell the story entrusted to us.

It may be helpful to ask two questions as we think about how the Christian community might adjust its speech to the reality of its minority status. What tone of voice most irritates people, and why? And how can we speak with both conviction and humility?

Embracing

The Christian community is now a minority in Western societies, whether we like this or not. If we are to thrive in this new context, we will need to make adjustments to our thinking, speaking and practice. This chapter has done no more than sample some of them. These are challenging times and we will require discernment, humility and courage as we make this journey. But minority status is not a cause for despair. There are very real advantages, if we have eyes to see them. Unencumbered by Saul's impressive armour, we can walk around more freely and find the far less impressive but much more useful resources we need to face the future, whether or not a Goliath stands in our path.

But might we go further and 'embrace' minority status? This is quite different from grudging acceptance or resentful adjustment. Embracing implies passion, enjoyment and enthusiastic commitment.

This may seem counterintuitive, irresponsible or defeatist. If the gospel of Jesus Christ is the good news of God's kingdom for all people (and indeed all of creation), we cannot be content with minority status, can we? Reflecting on the early church's transition from minority to majority status following imperial support and endorsement, William Cavanaugh writes: 'The minority status of the early church is not normative: it is *not* the way God wants it to be. God wants the whole world to be evangelized.'[22]

But this global ambition does not mean that minority status cannot be God's intention for the Christian community in some places and at some times. As we have seen, there are numerous examples in the biblical narrative of God choosing to work through minorities and leading his people into contexts where they were minorities. One of the classic Old Testament instances is the winnowing of Gideon's army so that credit for its stunning victory over the Midianites would go to God rather than Israel and would lead to renewed faith in God.[23] A minority community is less tempted to attribute success to its own resources and strategies. Majority status can be deeply problematic. The Christian community has generally behaved badly and oppressively when in the majority. Certainly, the accelerated transition from minority to majority status in the fourth and fifth centuries that imperial endorsement achieved had many pernicious consequences. If the minority Christian community had continued to grow without

[22] William Cavanaugh, 'What Constantine Has to Teach Us', in *Constantine Revisited* (ed. John Roth; Eugene, OR: Pickwick, 2013), p. 91.
[23] Judg. 7:2–7.

this endorsement and subsequent pressurized conversions, it might have more slowly become a more authentic and much less oppressive majority.

Embracing minority status does not mean abandoning hope for global evangelization or for the transformation of our own neighbourhood or nation. It means discerning the purposes of God, heeding Jesus' response to his disciples asking when the kingdom would arrive – 'it is not for you to know the times or periods that the Father has set by his own authority'[24] – and celebrating the opportunities that minority status offers.

As well as embracing minority *status*, we might also embrace the *process* of transition from majority to minority status. This process is painful and disorientating but full of potential. It has been described by several writers, who draw on the insights of cultural anthropologists, as a 'liminal' space. Liminality is a threshold experience, an unsettling time that poses questions about former assumptions and practices, strips away what we have previously relied on, and invites us courageously to embrace a new paradigm and new possibilities.[25]

It has been encouraging to discover examples of this in recent months. David Kerrigan, the general director of BMS World Mission, wonders if the church of the future will be different: 'Having less power and influence might make us kinder, a people characterised by grace and hope while remaining confident in the truths we proclaim.' He envisions 'a church committed to an incarnational "living out" of the gospel alongside its proclamation'.[26] Another BMS publication reported a comment made by Philip Richardson, the archbishop of New Zealand, who said that the decline in the number of Christians in his country 'liberates us from notions of self-importance and turns us back to our fundamental calling'.[27]

Perhaps the rising generation will have a different perspective on minority status from those who have some memory of being a

---

[24] Acts 1:7.

[25] An early example of this application of insights from cultural anthropology is Alan Roxburgh, *The Missionary Congregation, Leadership, and Liminality* (New York: Continuum, 1997).

[26] Writing in *Mission Catalyst* 2 (2014), p. 2.

[27] *Engage* (Spring 2014), p. 5.

majority (or at least assuming they still were). Miriam Swaffield of the Christian student organization, Fusion, writes:

> Less than one per cent of students can be accounted for who actively follow Jesus, and the 'millennial generation' is known as 'the missing generation' from our churches. Yes, we are a minority, but that means that those who stand up and follow the way of Jesus, against the tide of the majority, really have to know what they're living for. We can't do cultural Christianity because it's not in our culture anymore and we can't just go along with it because our friends are, because they aren't. I wonder if there isn't a gift in it being hard and costly to be a Christian in my generation, because maybe those of us who are know the reality of what we have signed up to for life?[28]

Weighing up the pros and cons of being a minority community and recognizing that there are significant liberties and opportunities may help us make the necessary adjustments. If we are to seize these opportunities and revel in these liberties, however, we will need to forsake our love affair with cultural domination and whole-heartedly embrace our new status. For many in the Christian community this further step may take some time, and it is important that this is not rushed. Rushing headlong into relationships and becoming intimate with those we hardly know is one of the less appealing and more dehumanizing aspects of contemporary culture. If 'love is patient and kind',[29] those of us who are enthusiastic about the changed landscape and eager to explore it will not pressurize others to run alongside us. In the end, an authentic and loving embrace of minority status will be the outcome of trusting God's reassurance that 'I know the plans I have for you . . . plans for your welfare and not for harm, to give you a future with hope'.[30]

---

[28] Writing in *The Bible in Transmission* (Winter 2013), p. 15.
[29] See 1 Cor. 13:4.
[30] Jer. 29:11.

4.

Sustaining and Resourcing

Forming, Nurturing and Sustaining

The Christian community is now a minority in a culture that no longer embraces its values, shares its vision, knows its story or can offer much in the way of encouragement to those who want to follow Jesus. This may seem obvious, but most churches are only just starting to wrestle with the implications. Dwight Friesen of the Seattle School of Theology writes,

> The church within post-Christendom contexts has just begun to notice that it has few, if any, secular teammates committed to forming Christian missional identity, which means that the church must reimagine how to fulfil its God-given mission to form holistic Christian identity without the aid of public institutions. One of the great ironies is that Christian identity formation within Christendom was far more holistic than it is today, in the sense that nearly all aspects of life were being intentionally and theologically constructed so as to weave a tapestry of Christian belief in the hearts, minds and actions of individual persons within the Christendom nations. Do not hear me suggesting that we must return to Christendom; we must not (even if we could), for life in the way of Christ cannot and should not be legislated . . .Today the weight of Christian missional formation rests squarely on the shoulders of the local church.[1]

Some might argue that this weight can be shared by other institutions and communities, such as Christian families, Christian

[1] Dwight Friesen, in *The Gospel after Christendom* (ed. Ryan Bolger; Grand Rapids: Baker, 2012), pp. 197–8.

schools, new monastic communities, mission agencies and other extra-congregational groups. But the issue of 'Christian identity formation' is crucial as we transition from majority to minority status, and undoubtedly much will depend on the readiness and capacity of local churches to be much more intentional about this. So we need to return to the issue of sustainability. While we must simplify church life and invest energy only in what we can sustain, we must also consider what a minority community needs to form its identity, sustain its life and resource its members so that it can thrive in this new context.

Simplifying is one aspect of the reconfiguring of church life that has been underway since at least the late 1990s. Although various terms used to describe this process – 'emerging church', 'new ways of being church', 'fresh expressions of church' and others – are not fully interchangeable, they are all indicative of ferment within, on the edge of and beyond existing churches. The Christian community is searching for ways of being church that are appropriate in a changed and changing culture, in which it is now a minority. Some of these experimental initiatives have been intriguing but short-lived. Some have been self-indulgent and reactive. Some have adopted ready-made models that have 'worked' elsewhere, rather than engaging in cultural and missional reflection. Some are not as radical as they think they are. And some might be harbingers of ways of being church that will flourish in the coming decades. Critics from within the Christian community have found ways of dismissing and denigrating them. Some observers from beyond the Christian community have suggested they are the last desperate efforts of a dying institution. Some reports have indicated that they are effective in connecting with people beyond the reach of more traditional churches, although the evidence is not yet fully persuasive. But there are thousands of such initiatives across Western culture representing, whatever their weaknesses, an explosion of creative, courageous and contextual missiology. And many are embracing a less institutional and simpler form of church.[2]

These developments, and especially various attempts to stream-line and simplify church life, have not surprisingly stimulated

---

[2] The terms 'simple church' and 'organic church' have been used to describe some of these initiatives, but the trend towards simplifying church life is broader than this.

passionate discussion about what is and is not essential. What is 'the ecclesial minimum'? Or, more generally, 'What do we mean by "church"?' This has been the topic of numerous conferences, online discussions, books and conversations in recent years. No agreement has been reached, but meanwhile another question that may be more fundamental has become more urgent: 'How do we make disciples?' Jesus told us to go and make disciples, some argue, and assured us that he would build his church.[3] Maybe, if we concentrate on forming, nurturing and resourcing disciples, we will be better able to discern the essential features of church life. Reimagining and reforming the Christian community, simplifying church structures and processes, contextualizing our missional engagement with a diverse and fluid culture – these are all important tasks, but we dare not neglect the issue of discipleship and how a minority community sustains and equips its members.

Discipleship

Discipleship is a familiar word within the Christian community and we need not over-define or over-complicate what we are talking about. Other words sometimes used as equivalents to disciples are 'apprentices', 'followers' or 'learners'. Maybe we should make no distinction between 'believers' and 'disciples', especially if, as some New Testament scholars argue,[4] 'believers' really means 'loyalists', whose primary allegiance is to Christ and his kingdom. It is certainly not helpful to imply that 'disciples' are on a higher level than mere 'believers' or that any member of the Christian community has either achieved this status or is exempt from bothering about it. Discipleship is the vocation of all who respond to the invitation of Jesus to 'follow me', and the Christian community is the context within which we learn and follow. Forming, sustaining and resourcing disciples, then, are foundational tasks of the Christian community, regardless of whether it is a majority or minority community, and whatever fresh expressions of this community might be emerging.

---

[3] Matt. 28:19 and Matt. 16:18.

[4] For example, Gordon Zerbe, *Citizenship: Paul on Peace and Politics* (Winnipeg: CMU Press, 2012).

So what is provoking the discussion about discipleship in many circles? What is causing the widespread angst about this? Why are some speaking about a 'crisis' of discipleship?[5] There seem to be several interlocking factors:

- Surveys indicate that there is often little difference in the lifestyles and priorities of those who claim to be Christians and those who do not. Although this finding might be explained away on the grounds that such surveys often do not differentiate between nominal Christians and those who participate actively in the Christian community, we would do well to take this seriously.[6] The point is not that we should expect Muslims, secularists or others inevitably to be less ethical than Christians (any such assumption or attempt to claim the moral high ground understandably causes outrage, especially in light of the past behaviour of the Christian community as a majority). But our lives as followers of Jesus are (or should be) shaped by a different story that summons us to different loyalties and commitments. In a challenging phrase attributed to former archbishop of Paris, Emmanuel Suhard, the mark of discipleship is 'to live in such a way that one's life would not make sense if God did not exist'.[7] But our churches are struggling to nurture us as counter-cultural disciples whose lives are attractive and question-posing. The moral failures of church leaders and high-profile Christians may make juicy headlines, but more enervating are our daily compromises and cultural collusions that do nothing to encourage our friends and neighbours to investigate the faith we proclaim. We need to take personal responsibility for this, but we also need help to be faithful disciples and effective witnesses.
- Recent surveys also reveal high levels of biblical illiteracy. Our foundational story is not well known and the biblical text is not shaping our lives, inspiring faithfulness or challenging unfaithfulness. In many churches only small snippets

---

[5] See, for example, Lucy Peppiatt, *The Disciple* (Eugene, OR: Cascade, 2012), p. xiii.

[6] See further Eddie Gibbs, *The Rebirth of the Church* (Grand Rapids: Baker, 2013), pp. 151ff.

[7] Quoted in Lee Griffith, *The Fall of the Prison* (Grand Rapids: Eerdmans, 1993), p. 180.

are read, worship is largely devoid of biblical narrative, and there is no opportunity to grasp the 'big story' that Scripture tells. Furthermore, many members of the Christian community do not open their Bibles from one Sunday to the next and so are dependent on this meagre fare. Nigel Wright claims: 'Levels of biblical literacy among Christian people are likely at the present time to be lower than they have been since the invention of the printing press.'[8] This is as true in churches committed to a high view of Scripture as others.[9]

- Studies also reveal that many Christians feel ill-equipped for discipleship in daily life, because their churches are not resourcing and equipping them to be faithful followers of Jesus in other spheres of life than their congregational involvement. There is little teaching, reflection or encouragement in relation to discipleship at work, at home, in leisure activities, or other dimensions of private and public life.[10]

- There has been an alarming exodus from our churches, many of them Christians of long standing, who have stagnated in their faith, are burnt out by over-demanding and unsustainable programmes and are not finding the resources they need to grow or be sustained as disciples. Rather than blaming them for leaving or ignoring them, maybe we need to listen carefully to their experiences.

- In the Christendom era, there was less of a gap between church and culture. An hour of worship and preaching on a Sunday seemed adequate to resource churchgoers for the rest of the week, especially when discipleship was understood as being compliant citizens and conforming to cultural norms. But this understanding is inappropriate for a minority community in a plural culture, and we cannot assume that what happens on a Sunday morning, or whenever churches meet, is adequate, especially if this experience is largely passive.

---

[8] Nigel Wright, *New Baptists, New Agenda* (Carlisle: Paternoster, 2002), p. 25.

[9] See, for example, http://www.lifeway.com/Article/research-survey-bible-engagement-churchgoers; http://poncefoundation.com/project/christians-dont-read-their-bible.

[10] See further Michael Frost, *Incarnate: The Body of Christ in an Age of Disengagement* (Downers Grove: IVP, 2014), pp. 132–47.

Faithful discipleship does not imply cultural conformity. On the contrary, if we are now a minority community, discipleship will often mean nonconformity and counter-cultural priorities and practices. This is, at least in part, what David Augsburger, professor of pastoral care and counselling at Fuller Theological Seminary, means by 'dissident discipleship'.[11] There will, of course, be aspects of our culture that we do not dissent from but gladly affirm. Some of these may be more consistent with gospel values than the supposedly Christian culture of the Christendom era, and we should acknowledge this. But we will need to be more intentional about practices that encourage and resource a more discerning and more courageous form of discipleship.

And we will need to do this in a cultural context where there is plenty of discipling taking place, promoting and advocating different values, ambitions and practices. Several years ago, Graham Cray, until recently chair of Fresh Expressions, and I spoke at the launch of the Church of Scotland's 'Emerging Ministries' venture. I remember Graham insisting that we live in a 'discipling culture' and explaining the challenges this presents. We live in a highly contested environment. Around us are corporations, political parties, economists, interest groups, advertisers and others with huge resources and great expertise in discipling us into ways they want us to think, react and behave. The skills of cultural discipling (indoctrination, propaganda, manipulation) have been finely honed and are now highly effective and largely undetected. We are catechized daily by the advertising industry, the films we watch, the books we read, the news channels we rely on and television programmes we enjoy. Some of this discipling is subtle and insidious, but even that which is initially disturbing can infiltrate our thinking as we are gradually numbed through repetition. And we are expected to conform to the dominant world-view and its priorities and values. We are under pressure. Discipling in the Christian community cannot take place in isolation from this or disregard the power of this cultural discipling.

Before we examine some practices that might help us respond to this challenge, we will highlight various ways of understanding discipleship.

---

[11] David Augsburger, *Dissident Discipleship* (Grand Rapids: Brazos, 2006).

Imago Dei: Becoming Human

One of my regular teaching commitments is the Crucible course, which has been running in Birmingham each year since 2005. Designed primarily to equip those who are pioneering or planning to pioneer, especially in urban communities, one of the teaching weekends explores issues of discipleship under the rubric of 'becoming human'. We have found this language a refreshing and helpful way of grappling with various dimensions of discipleship.[12]

We quote with relish pithy statements from two famous Christian leaders. Irenaeus declares: 'The glory of God is seen in a human life fully lived', and Dietrich Bonhoeffer advises: 'We should give up the foolish task of trying to be saints and get on with the more important task of being fully human.' We point participants to Jean Vanier's remarkable book, *Becoming Human*, in which he reflects on his experiences among people with learning difficulties.[13] And we ponder the meaning of *imago Dei* and the implications for mission and discipleship of recognizing that we ourselves and all those we encounter are made in God's image.

We examine dehumanizing features of the 'discipling culture' that surrounds us, identifying these and reflecting on their influence. We note the caricatures and stereotypes that diminish our individuality and our capacity to relate humanly with others. We gather examples of the kind of language that dehumanizes us: 'consumers', 'clients', 'human resources', 'service-users', 'ordinary people', 'collateral damage'. We acknowledge that we sometimes succumb to the temptation to treat each other as means, rather than ends, such as when we engage in 'networking' instead of authentic relating. And we spend time critiquing the advertising

---

[12] See http://www.cruciblecourse.org.uk.

[13] Jean Vanier, *Becoming Human* (London: Darton, Longman & Todd, 1999). It is interesting also to note that Lucy Peppiatt's book on discipleship is subtitled 'On Becoming Truly Human' and that Leonard Hjalmerson, in *Text and Context: Church Planting in Canada in Post-Christendom* (Portland, OR: Urban Loft, 2013), reports (p. 22) that the question 'What does it mean to be truly human?' has been just beneath the surface of most of the discussions he has had in recent years with missional pioneers.

industry that plays on our struggles with self-worth and manipulates our desires and values.

During the weekend we study the life of Jesus as the fully human one and ask what it means to follow him and become more fully human ourselves. We note that Western Christians have historically struggled to take the full humanity of Jesus seriously. This was especially so after the Christendom shift in the fourth century. Once the church had attained majority status and was becoming increasingly conformed to values and practices that were alien to the New Testament, the life and teachings of Jesus became embarrassing and troublesome. To their credit, the churches held on to the conviction that Jesus was fully human as well as fully God, despite the difficulty of understanding and stating the relationship between his divinity and humanity, but they gave little attention to his humanity.

This is clear from the ecumenical creeds, which say almost nothing about his human life and move straight from Christmas to Easter. The Nicene Creed, for instance, follows 'born of the Virgin Mary' with 'suffered under Pontius Pilate'. The life of Jesus – his lifestyle, teaching, miracles, conversations, encounters and priorities – is reduced to a comma. Why is this? No creed can cover everything and these creeds were formulated to address the issues facing the churches in the fourth and fifth centuries. But why was the life and teaching of Jesus of so little interest in this period? Over the next several centuries the church struggled to know how to interpret and apply the teaching of Jesus, which now seemed idealistic and too demanding in a context where Christianity had become conventional rather than counter-cultural.

Within and outside the mainstream, however, minority movements, such as the Franciscans, the Waldensians and the Anabaptists, rediscovered the Jesus of the gospels and insisted that his life is the pattern for ours. He is the example we are to follow. His teachings are to be obeyed. Just as he is the image of God in human flesh, so we are to be conformed to his image. We are to be disciples who respond to his commission – 'as the Father has sent me, so I send you' (John 20:21).

We recognize that there are dangers in movements like these that emphasize following Jesus:

- Legalism – following rules rather than following Jesus;
- Selectivity – choosing which aspects of the life and teaching of Jesus to emphasize;
- Activism – we are to be 'human beings, not human doings';
- Perfectionism – often coupled with low self-esteem and criticism of others; and
- Self-reliance – rather than relying on the Holy Spirit for grace and power.

But, if we are aware of these dangers and look to the Spirit as the one whose mission (John 20:22) is to empower and humanize us, then learning from and becoming more like Jesus, the fully human being, the image of the invisible God, is the path to becoming truly human.

We have found that the language of 'becoming human' helps us avoid over-spiritualizing the idea of discipleship, endorsing a sacred/secular divide, or relating discipleship too closely to church activities. In too many churches the emphasis appears to be on producing loyal and active church members rather than equipping each other for whole-life discipleship. This we want to resist. In some others, discipleship seems to be interpreted as life-denying rather than life-enhancing, restricting rather than liberating, a long way from Jesus' promise of 'life in all its fullness'. The language of 'becoming human' invites us to participate in the adventure of becoming all that God wants us to be. And responses from participants in this course (and in other contexts) suggest that many have found this understanding of discipleship helpful.

Missio Dei: Whole-Life Discipleship

If the language of 'becoming human' points away from a narrow focus on personal morality and spirituality or loyal and active church involvement and towards whole-life discipleship, setting discipleship in the context of *missio Dei* enhances this. The concept of *missio Dei*, familiar to theologians and missiologists for several decades, has only recently become more widely known in the Christian community, and its ramifications are still being worked through. We will explore this concept further in Chapter 6, but here we note its implications for our understanding of discipleship.

Missio Dei insists that mission starts not with the Christian community but with God and that we are invited to participate in this divine initiative. *Missio Dei* alerts us to the scope of God's mission, which is multifaceted, multidimensional and all-embracing. It is the 'big story' of the Bible.[14] It is the full realization of all that is meant by the prophetic vision of *shalom*, the answer to the prayer of God's people through the centuries: 'Your will be done, your kingdom come on earth as in heaven.'

Those who respond to the invitation to participate in God's mission, then, are involved in all kinds of activities that anticipate the fulfilment of God's purposes: evangelism, working for justice, care for creation, church planting, political activism, education, reconciling enemies, cultural renewal, healing minds and bodies, offering hope and imagination.

If this is the scope of God's mission, the scope of discipleship is equally broad. Participating in the mission of God involves every member of the Christian community living as a disciple in all walks of life and in every dimension of our lives. Participating in the mission of God is not the subject of one session in a discipleship course, but the framework for all aspects of discipleship. The Christian community needs to form and resource disciples who can engage in diverse expressions of mission in our families, neighbourhoods, workplaces, relational networks and spheres of voluntary service.

This does not mean that every disciple or every Christian community can be involved in all these dimensions of mission. A minority community, however vast, needs to be realistic and focused. Hyperactivity does not equate to being missional and soon becomes unsustainable. Unduly busy church programmes can hinder whole-life discipleship, isolate us from others, and distract us from engaging in authentic mission. Individuals and churches need to discern their particular vocation within the broad scope of God's mission.

It is probably best to resist the temptation to call this 'missional discipleship', as if there were any other authentic expression of

[14] See Christopher Wright, *The Mission of God: Unlocking the Bible's Grand Narrative* (Downers Grove: IVP, 2006).

discipleship (just as 'missional church' is an oxymoron and is helpful only as a corrective to a centuries-long disjunction between church and mission that has been deeply damaging to both). Neither mission nor discipleship is a specialized activity. Our vocation is to be whole-life disciples who are learning to be more available to the God of mission, more attentive to what the Spirit is doing and saying, and more alert to opportunities we encounter in our daily lives. This whole-life discipleship, of course, includes personal spirituality, consistent behaviour and participation in the Christian community that sustains us, but the overarching framework of *missio Dei* protects us from self-absorbed and institutional interpretations of discipleship.

Stories and Reflexes

The separation of church and mission was not ubiquitous during the Christendom era. The minority movements mentioned above (and others) reflected deeply on the human life of Jesus and developed community practices to form and sustain disciples. They also regarded participation in God's mission as the calling of all members of the community. This was certainly true of the sixteenth-century Anabaptists, a missional movement that had distinctive discipling practices. The Anabaptists were profoundly shaped by stories. As a movement persecuted by both Catholics and Protestants, many of their cherished stories are martyr stories. Rehearsing these stories and reflecting on their implications has sustained them as a minority community that has only recently, after centuries of misrepresentation, begun to be rehabilitated. It is from Anabaptism and other minority Christian communities that Christians today are learning as we adjust to the minority status that those movements have experienced for much longer.

We should not underestimate the power of stories to shape communities, sustain faith and inspire discipleship. This is one of the reasons why biblical illiteracy and ignorance of the narratives of Scripture and the big story the Bible tells is so debilitating. Our communities also need to tell more recent stories, local stories, and stories from our own lives (the much neglected practice of 'testimony'). If the Christian community is to maintain its identity and have anything to offer as a creative minority in a plural and contested culture, we will need to know the story of which we are a part, tell fresh stories that encourage renewed faithfulness, and out-narrate the stories that shape the surrounding culture. Reflecting on the inspirational role played by storytelling in the classic adventure novel *Watership Down*, theologian and ethicist Stanley Hauerwas concludes: 'The most basic task of any polity is to offer its people a sense of participation in an adventure. For finally what we seek is not power, or security, or equality, or even dignity, but a sense of worth gained from participation and contribution to a common adventure.'[15]

Probably the most famous Anabaptist story is that of Dirk Willems, a young man in Asperen in the Netherlands in the second half of the sixteenth century. It is a poignant story that has been told and retold, illustrated and dramatized, a story that provokes discussion, a story about reflexes.[16]

Dirk, who belonged to a proscribed Anabaptist community, was arrested and imprisoned in 1569 to await trial and likely execution. Somehow, he escaped and ran for his life across the fields and onto a frozen canal. But the alarm was raised and he was pursued by a prison guard as he stepped out onto the ice. Perhaps he was rather thin after time in prison; the ice held as Dirk ran across, but the better-fed guard felt the ice crack and he slipped into the freezing water. This was Dirk's opportunity to make good his escape, but instead he turned back and rescued the guard, pulling him to the shore. Others had by now arrived and Dirk was promptly rearrested and confined in a more secure prison. He was subsequently burned at the stake for heresy.

Anabaptists and others have reflected deeply on this story, asking various questions. Why did Dirk turn back? Was he right to do this, or should he have escaped? What would I have done in this situation? What is clear is that Dirk's choice was a reflex action. There was no time to sit down and weigh up the options, debate the ethical issues involved, consult his pastor or wait for a sermon on the subject. His act of mercy was instinctive. We do not

[15] Stanley Hauerwas, *A Community of Character* (Notre Dame: University of Notre Dame Press, 1981), p. 13.

[16] See David Luthy, *Dirk Willems: His Noble Deed Lives On* (Aylmer, ON: Pathway Publishers, 2011).

know whether he later regretted it or was at peace with his decision, but his reflex action was to rescue his pursuer, to save that man's life at the cost of his own.

Reflecting on this story poses another question. Who or what had shaped Dirk's reflexes? We know little about Dirk's underground community in Asperen, but the Anabaptist tradition has placed huge emphasis on the Sermon on the Mount and especially Jesus' teaching about love of enemies. It is likely that Dirk had internalized this to such an extent that his reflex action on the ice was to turn back and save his enemy. Reflexes are nurtured in communities that consistently teach and model distinctive virtues and values.

A much more recent, but equally poignant, story on which Anabaptists and others have been reflecting is the response of the Amish community to the shooting of several young girls in Nickel Mines, Pennsylvania, in October 2006 by a lone gunman who then killed himself. The world's media expressed shock, not only at the tragedy itself, but at the speed with which the community expressed forgiveness for the perpetrator. Some were offended, judging that this must be superficial, but moved on before discovering that members of the community visited the gunman's distraught mother, attended her son's funeral and shared with her some of the money raised in response to this tragedy.[17]

This story raises similar questions to that of Dirk Willems. Why did the Amish community so quickly, reflexively, express forgiveness despite their deep grief? Was this the right response? What would I have done in this situation? And the deeper question again: What shaped their reflexes so that they responded in this way? This community, like Dirk's, meditated often on the Sermon on the Mount, nurtured reflexes of loving their enemies and deeply imbibed the commitment to forgiveness at the heart of the Lord's Prayer.

Not all stories from the Anabaptist tradition are as impressive or disturbing as these, for the Anabaptist community is as flawed as any other. And other traditions have their own stories that need to be heard and pondered. Stories shape communities and form us as disciples. And stories like these encourage us to think

---

[17] On the Nickel Mines incident, see Donald Kraybill et al., *Amish Grace: How Forgiveness Transcended Tragedy* (San Francisco: Jossey-Bass, 2007).

of discipleship as re-reflexing and to ask, not what we say we believe, or how we think we should live, but what kind of people are we? How do we respond under pressure, when we have no time to think things through? Not what rules does our community teach, but what kind of reflexes is our community nurturing in us? Minority communities, if they are to thrive, will nurture a range of counter-cultural reflexes.

Communities of Discernment and Resistance

American theologian Walter Wink concluded his exhaustive study of the language of power in the New Testament with a book subtitled 'Discernment and Resistance in a World of Domination'.[18] Interpreting the 'principalities and powers' as a 'domination system' that oppresses humanity and hinders the mission of God, he calls the Christian community to develop skills of discernment and resistance. This is not something a majority community with vested interests in the status quo can easily do, but it comes much more naturally to a minority community – once it has accepted this status. And this double task of discerning and resisting is for communities, rather than individuals.

The approaches to discipleship we have explored all emphasize the role of the community. It is in the community, not in isolation, that we become more fully human. It is the community, not just individuals, that participates in the multifaceted mission of God. And the community is the context within which stories are rehearsed and reflexes are developed. The struggle to be faithful disciples in a society that promotes a very different vision and champions values and practices that are contrary to the gospel is not one that we are meant to engage in alone.

We live in a culture that yearns for authentic community but insists on the rights and liberties of individuals and resists any significant intrusion into our personal space and any challenges to our beliefs and commitments. And this individualism is evident in our churches, with our seating arrangements that hinder interaction, monologue sermons that preclude participation, the practice of

---

[18] Walter Wink, *Engaging the Powers: Discernment and Resistance in a World of Domination* (Minneapolis: Fortress Press, 1992).

tithing that needs no conversations about lifestyle, and our instinctive distaste for any kind of accountability processes.

This is not new. John Bunyan's classic tale, *The Pilgrim's Progress*, describes an individual journey of discipleship. Pilgrim has companions from time to time, but this is the journey of a heroic individual and his struggle to be faithful and keep his eyes fixed on the heavenly city to which he is travelling. Many other spiritual classics similarly encourage personal growth and development with little or no reference to the role of companions or the community.[19]

Not that this is entirely wrong. An important aspect of becoming disciples is taking personal responsibility for the way we live and not placing undue reliance on others – 'self-propelling disciples', as Church Army researcher George Lings memorably designates this. Some of us are unhealthily dependent on church services, sermons from our favourite preachers, pastoral counselling, conferences and support groups. And some congregations and organizations encourage this, failing to discern the powerful influence of the therapeutic culture within contemporary society and creating dependency instead of resourcing responsible discipleship. In 2007, the Willow Creek Community Church, which has influenced so many churches, acknowledged this and lamented that they had not helped people to 'take responsibility to become self-feeders'.[20]

But independence is no healthier than dependence. The New Testament frequently uses 'one another' phrases to encourage interdependence and mutuality. We need each other's support but we also have gifts and insights to offer each other as fellow-pilgrims, companions on the journey of discipleship. We need to belong to communities of discernment and resistance in which we participate actively, both giving and receiving.

A community of discernment and resistance refuses either to be isolated from or co-opted by the society in which it is set. It reminds

[19] For an alternative approach, see J. Nelson Kraybill, *On the Pilgrim's Way* (Scottdale: Herald Press, 1997), in which the author records his conversations on discipleship with various walking companions.

[20] The research is presented and analysed in Greg Hawkins and Cally Parkinson, *Reveal: Where Are You?* (Chicago: Willow Creek Association, 2007).

its members of its founding story, celebrates this in worship and explores its implications for discipleship. But it also listens carefully to the other stories that are shaping its society, examines their assumptions, exposes their ideologies and unmasks contemporary idols. Discernment means recognizing and affirming what is good and deserving of support as well as identifying malign and dehumanizing influences that call for resistance. This is the prophetic role of the Christian community and our pastoral responsibility to each other as we share and test our insights, equipping each other to reflect theologically on family, work, society, study, leisure activities, local community and global issues – asking how we can live as faithful disciples in all spheres of life.

The fragmented nature of the Christian community means that on many issues there is likely to be disagreement, and so discernment will be provisional and resistance only patchy. Many centuries of collusion with and investment in the 'domination system' means that discerning and resisting by an ex-majority community will involve repentance and internal reorientation as well as critique of contemporary values and practices. And, as noted in an earlier chapter, there are other minority communities in our society with their own stories and priorities; they too will engage in discernment and resistance. The Christian community, if we will, can learn much from these communities, even if we will not always share their perspectives. Humility, then, and openness to fresh insights will be important dimensions of the task of discernment and resistance. And in a plural and evolving society, this is a never-ending task.

Discipleship Practices

Intentionality is at the heart of discipleship in a minority community. This is not to discount the many informal ways in which we learn to be followers of Jesus – through watching and learning from others, conversations with friends, reading good books, sharing our faith in word and deed, and participating in the rhythm of life of the Christian community. But it is clear from widespread concern about how disciples are formed and sustained that this is not enough. We need to be more intentional about being disciples and helping one another on the journey. And we need to go beyond merely challenging each other to be disciples, to offer each other practical help and resources.

Weary church leaders may be reluctant to read any further. But intentionality is about clarity and focus, not extra activities that add further demands. A community may need to review its activities and ensure that these really do nurture disciples, discontinuing those that do not and sharpening those that remain so that their potential is maximized. This may then release time and energy for introducing new and more helpful activities.

Since preaching plays such a significant role in many Christian communities, examining the relationship between preaching and discipleship might be a helpful place to begin. There are many ways in which preaching has the capacity to nurture disciples: rehearsing the big story the Bible tells; helping the community learn how to interpret their Scriptures; demonstrating how to apply biblical teaching to contemporary issues; challenging assumptions, values and priorities; bringing reassurance of God's love and good purposes; encouraging faithful and courageous nonconformity; reviving hope and vision; and so on. But maybe the link between preaching and discipleship needs to be more explicit and intentional. Research indicates, worryingly, that much preaching is ineffectual – not because the sermons are poor or the preachers are dull, but because not enough is done to help listeners follow through on what we hear. There are many ways of addressing this: inviting questions and comments on the sermons so that the whole community is actively engaged; preaching fewer sermons and spending much more time reflecting together on the implications of what has been preached; and encouraging one another to report on ways we have applied what we have heard. For it is application, and not just listening to sermons, that forms Christian identity. Preaching is not meant to be a stand-alone activity, but a resource for a learning community.

In the gatherings of many Christian communities a disproportionate amount of time is spent singing. Some of the songs express praise and thanksgiving to God. Others are sung prayers or express the desires and commitments of members of the community. The songs we sing have the capacity to touch us deeply, shape our priorities, transform our perspectives and encourage faithful discipleship. It may be true that our theology is derived more from the songs we sing than the sermons we hear. So it is vital that we give attention to what we are – and are not – singing. If the language is banal, the subject matter is restricted and repetitive, the focus is individualistic, the mood is unvarying, and the narrative dimension is lacking, what we sing may contribute little to the task of resourcing discipleship – especially if what we sing is not integrated into other aspects of worship and learning.

Nor is it appropriate for a minority community, however vast, to sing triumphalist hymns or songs that sound hollow in their inflated expectations. Celebrating the lordship of Christ and anticipating the coming of God's kingdom is appropriately subversive worship as long as we recognize its political implications, the unconventional nature of Christ's lordship, and how our commitment to his kingdom relativizes other loyalties and undermines the priorities and expectations of contemporary culture. Paul Roberts, tutor at Trinity College, Bristol, notes some encouraging developments: 'Alternative worship seems to be embarking upon a long-term project of replacing the doxology of the triumphant church of Christendom, with all its questionable allegiances. To do this, emerging worship practices need to find words of praise that eschew aspiration for a kingdom of human worldly power, by discovering again the exuberant and heavenly praise of the deviants and those whom the world has marginalised.'[21]

And do we really need to sing so many songs? Could we not explore other ways of glorifying God and expressing our praise and worship? Preaching and singing in many churches eats up an inordinate amount of time. Not only do these activities dominate time spent together, but preachers spend hours preparing sermons each week, musicians and worship leaders spend further hours rehearsing together, and technicians spend yet more hours on sophisticated sound systems and audiovisual technology. Do the benefits repay this investment of time and energy? Many emerging churches are unconvinced and are exploring alternative forms of worship and learning, and the questions they are asking resonate with inherited churches too. Might fewer monologue sermons, fewer songs and a simpler approach to church enable us to become less stressed, more

[21] Paul Roberts in Bolger, *Gospel after Christendom*, p. 185.

creative and better able to develop practices that do more to sustain and resource disciples?

What might these practices be? There is no shortage of books available on discipleship and Christian formation. The Christian community has access to many 'discipleship courses', some home-grown and contextual, others produced by organizations or denominations and marketed as effective in every context. Despite the undoubted merits of these courses, the widespread concern about discipleship suggests there are also serious deficiencies. Many seem unduly focused on doctrine – ensuring we believe correctly – or church life – ensuring that we belong properly. Less attention is paid to lifestyle, priorities and mission. Most are also individualistic and very short.

These problematic features are a legacy of what happened once the church had become a majority community. This had a profound impact on the early church's catechetical system – a lengthy process by which new members learned the way of discipleship and entered the church. This process was truncated as the system became overwhelmed by sheer weight of numbers and as minimal instruction was deemed sufficient in a changed context in which discipleship no longer meant nonconformity and the cultural Christianity that replaced it could be absorbed through osmosis. Now that we are once again a minority community, we may need to recover elements of the more rigorous approach that formed Christian disciples in the early centuries – a longer process of induction with cultural exorcisms, mentoring and patient instruction. And we will need to form communities that understand discipleship to be a lifelong process for 'followers of the Way' (as the early disciples were known before they were dubbed 'Christians').[22]

And there is some evidence that this is happening. The Catholic Neo-catechumenate (known also as 'The Way'), which has recently celebrated its fiftieth anniversary, encourages small groups to pursue ongoing Christian formation. Interest in contextualized forms of catechesis is growing in other traditions too.[23] The term

---

[22] Acts 9:2; 19:9, 23; 22:4.

[23] For example, Alan Kreider, 'Baptism and Catechesis as Spiritual Formation', in *Remembering our Future: Explorations in Deep Church* (ed. Andrew Walker and Luke Bretherton; Milton Keynes: Paternoster, 2007).

'new monasticism' has been coined to describe various communities that are exploring ways of re-appropriating ancient monastic traditions, including the novitiate, a rule of life and rhythms of prayer.[24] There has been renewed interest also in monastic wisdom on virtues and vices, the 'habits of the heart' that motivate us and shape our characters and choices. The vices are otherwise known as the 'seven deadly sins' and are usually trivialized or sensationalized in contemporary culture but monastic writings on these offer profound insights that move us well beyond the 'oughts' and 'shoulds' of many sermons.[25]

Other initiatives, such as the Lifeshapes programme developed by St Thomas Crookes in Sheffield,[26] Renovaré, which offers 'a practical strategy for spiritual formation',[27] and the Inspire Network, which aims to 'develop the spiritual life of mission-shaped disciples who abide deeply with God, and live missionally in the world',[28] are re-contextualizing spiritual disciplines that have been practised over the centuries. Many of these, unsurprisingly, require discipline and persistence, neither of which are popular qualities in a culture geared to instant gratification. But a minority community can choose to adopt a counter-cultural stance, resist the notion of short cuts, and encourage its members to embrace these disciplines and practise them patiently and consistently.

Some have also found helpful the notion of 'focal practices', a term coined by philosopher Albert Borgmann. Without denigrating the benefits of contemporary technologies, he argued that many devices make life easier rather than richer and advocated

---

[24] See Rutba House, *School(s) for Conversion: 12 Marks of a New Monasticism* (Eugene: Wipf & Stock, 2005).

[25] For example, Rebecca Konyndyk De Young, *Glittering Vices: A New Look at the Seven Deadly Sins and Their Remedies* (Ada, MI: Brazos Press, 2009). There are many more works on the virtues, including Stanley Hauerwas and Charles Pinches, *Christians Among the Virtues: Theological Conversations with Ancient and Modern Ethics* (Notre Dame: University of Notre Dame Press, 1997); and Tom Wright, *Virtue Reborn* (London: SPCK, 2010).

[26] See http://www.stthomaschurch.org.uk.

[27] See http://www.renovare.org.

[28] See http://inspiremovement.org.

lifestyle choices that are more demanding but more rewarding.[29] These might include learning to play an instrument rather than listening to music; cooking a meal together rather than ordering a takeaway; or building a log fire rather than switching on the central heating. Christian communities might be wary of indiscriminate use of technology and introduce focal practices that will encourage participation, build character and enrich their common life. What is needed, according to the authors of *Slow Church*, is an ecclesial equivalent of the 'slow food' movement and recovery of a currently unpopular virtue that was of central importance within the minority community of the early Christians – patience.[30]

These initiatives also advocate an approach to discipleship that involves companionship and mutual accountability. Perhaps the most potent aspect of the Lifeshapes programme is the 'huddle' – a small group that meets regularly to ask each other questions about discipleship. Its mantra is 'high accountability, low control'. Renovaré promotes and resources 'spiritual formation groups'. The Inspire Network draws inspiration from classic Methodist practices of accountability in small groups. And 'new monastic' communities value spiritual directors and soul friends. Our individualistic culture is not conducive to this level of accountability, but a minority community can choose to dissent from such individualism and recover the practices of mutual accountability that are taught in every strand of New Testament teaching, not least the classic passage in Matthew 18:15–17. This is not the most popular text in the gospels, but Jesus here sets out a process for addressing discipleship issues in the community. Historically, Anabaptists called this 'the rule of Christ' and at their baptisms committed themselves to this process. If we go astray, we need our brothers and sisters to help us get back on track. If we offend each other,

---

[29] See Albert Borgmann, *Technology and the Character of Contemporary Life: A Philosophical Inquiry* (Chicago: University of Chicago Press, 1984) and his subsequent writings. See also Arthur Boers, *Living into Focus: Choosing What Matters in an Age of Distractions* (Grand Rapids: Brazos, 2012).

[30] C. Christopher Smith and John Pattison, *Slow Church: Cultivating Community in the Patient Way of Jesus* (Downers Grove: IVP, 2014). See also Ian Stackhouse, *The Day is Yours: Slow Spirituality in a Fast-Moving World* (Milton Keynes: Paternoster, 2008).

we need to be held accountable and work towards the restoration of relationships. This forms a community in which discipleship is intentional and progressive.

A more intentional approach to forming and sustaining disciples will require churches to be more participative and multi-voiced than many currently are. The practices highlighted in this section involve personal disciplines but are set in the context of a supportive and accountable community. Other practices include: providing regular opportunities for theological reflection on issues of life and work as the Christian community listens to the experiences of members and dialogues with them; deconstructing film clips, television programmes or advertisements; more extensive public reading of Scripture so that we know and become immersed in the 'big story' the Bible tells; introducing an 'idol of the month' slot that encourages more nuanced cultural critique; and encouraging much greater use of contemporary testimonies that report and reflect on signs of God's kingdom throughout the week. The Imagine-Church initiative of the London Institute for Contemporary Christianity offers many other ideas and resources to equip the Christian community to encourage whole-life discipleship.[31]

The aim of these practices is to stimulate our imagination, to re-reflex us so that we respond in fresh ways, to re-narrate the world in line with God's mission, to help us develop 'habits of the heart', and to build communities that will nurture and sustain counter-cultural disciples. Australian missiologist Michael Frost writes: 'The struggle for Christians and church leaders is to explore what practices, liturgies or habits need to be cultivated in our lives to countermand the domination of ungodly pedagogies.'[32]

Such practices enable mutual learning and mature conversation rather than spoon-feeding, draw on the insights of many members of the community and encourage whole-life discipleship that resists any sacred/secular division. Such a multi-voiced environment, which is less reliant on preachers, pastors and worship leaders, is more likely to nurture disciples than one that breeds spectatorism, dependence and passivity. And multi-voiced church life stimulates whole-life discipleship. Active participants

[31] See http://www.licc.org.uk/imagine-church.

[32] Frost, *Incarnate*, p. 103.

in healthy multi-voiced churches are much more likely to be confident in sharing their faith with others, ready to engage in social action, hospitable to their neighbours, alert to pastoral opportunities beyond the church and able to participate in gracious dialogue and debate with people of other faiths or none.[33]

Money, Sex and Power

If we are not just interested in compliant church membership but committed to whole-life discipleship, we are confronted by a plethora of issues in a rapidly evolving cultural context. What does it mean to be faithful followers of Jesus today in all areas of life? And if we are not persuaded that we can simply adopt the conclusions reached by the Christian community when it was in the majority and tended to interpret Scripture in ways that did not threaten the status quo, we have work to do. We will, of course, value and learn from this heritage, but we may also dissent from it as we forge our identity as a minority Christian community in a very different cultural context. We will wrestle with issues previous generations faced and with issues they never imagined. We will be wary of being co-opted by the spirit of our age and its prevailing norms, but alert also to ways in which inherited views may themselves have been influenced by the cultural context in which they developed. Scripture will be our lodestone, but we will read this from a different perspective as a minority community.[34]

But where do we begin? How do we decide which issues require our attention most urgently or most often? Is the agenda set by the presenting issues in our local context or in the global context, or do we seize the opportunity as a minority community of exploring important but neglected issues on which we might make a distinctive contribution? Are there certain topics that we regard as definitive of faithfulness and approach with a line-in-the-sand stance, or do we concentrate on subjects that seem to be of greatest concern to the biblical writers?

---

[33] See further Stuart and Sian Murray Williams, *Multi-Voiced Church* (Milton Keynes: Paternoster, 2012).

[34] We will explore these wider issues further in the next chapter.

Issues relating to human sexuality (and especially homosexuality) have dominated the agenda in many sections of the Christian community in recent years. This is unsurprising given the importance of sexual relations to human beings in all generations, changing sexual norms and the preoccupation with sex in contemporary Western culture. On many of these issues there is no agreement as to how the biblical material should be interpreted, and there is deep concern within the Christian community about the implications of any conclusions reached for faithful discipleship and witness. Does a minority Christian community dissent from convictions held by most of its forebears and read Scripture in fresh ways as it becomes more sensitive to the experience of other minority communities and their treatment by a majority church? Or does it acknowledge past prejudice and oppression but nevertheless dissent from prevailing sexual norms and offer a counter-cultural perspective? And whichever approach different sections of the Christian community take, does this qualify as a line-in-the-sand issue?

It is often claimed that, however they are to be interpreted, there are very few biblical texts on the subject of homosexuality. This is not, of course, the whole picture as these texts must be read in the context of everything else Scripture says about sex, marriage, human relationships and the relationship between God and Israel or Christ and the church. Human sexuality is an important aspect of discipleship for the Christian community, and especially for a minority in a culture that is experiencing rapid changes in its approach to sexual ethics.

But it is doubtful that the Christian community should be as preoccupied with this subject as it has been. It is, after all, only one element of the classic triad of 'money, sex and power'.[35] There has been much greater reluctance to adopt a line-in-the-sand approach to issues of power and wealth – perhaps because of the very dubious heritage of a powerful and wealthy majority Christian community. But if weight of biblical material indicates the importance of a subject, we should be spending much more time exploring issues of discipleship in relation to money

---

[35] Many authors have written on this theme, prompting many series of sermons or Bible studies. One of the classics is Richard Foster, *Money, Sex and Power* (London: Hodder & Stoughton, 2009).

than in relation to sex.[36] The Bible says an enormous amount about money, wealth, poverty, possessions, economic principles and practices, giving and sharing. Someone has calculated that approximately one in every seven verses contributes something to this subject.

And contemporary Western culture is arguably more obsessed with money than with sex. The state of the economy and the perceived ability of politicians to manage this is the determining factor in most elections. The news media are dominated by economic issues and frequently assess the significance of all other issues – social, political, cultural, environmental – in terms of their economic ramifications. Materialism has inevitably increased as our society has given less credence to any spiritual dimension of life. Consumerism is rampant and shopping has become the leading leisure pursuit in many Western societies. The extent of biblical material on this issue, the contemporary obsession with money and goods, the level of individual and corporate debt, the incompatibility of the expectation of endless economic growth with the resources of a finite planet,[37] the very limited impact of the church in poor neighbourhoods, and the problematic legacy of a wealthy majority church together suggest that this should be a priority concern for a minority Christian community.

Perhaps we could focus on this specific, albeit wide-ranging, aspect of discipleship. Maybe if we learn to follow Jesus whole-heartedly in this area of our lives, the principles and practices we adopt will help us in other areas. After all, Mammon was the only spirit Jesus named, and he was clear that we face a stark choice between serving God or Mammon.[38] And if 'the love of money is a root of all kinds of evil',[39] finding freedom in this area of life might help us to live freely in many other areas. This does at least offer us a case study – an opportunity to apply the principles and practices outlined in this chapter to one dimension of discipleship.

---

[36] We will explore issues of power in a later chapter.

[37] Kenneth Boulding, an American Quaker and economist, famously said: 'Anyone who believes exponential growth can go on forever in a finite world is either a madman or an economist.' For resources on an alternative approach, see http://steadystate.org.

[38] Matt. 6:24.

[39] 1 Tim. 6:10.

We might begin by acknowledging that the majority Christian community has a very mixed track record in this area of discipleship and that for several centuries we have not practised the kind of economic discipleship we discover in the New Testament, in the early churches and in Christian communities elsewhere in the world. We might welcome the opportunity that becoming a minority community gives us to look afresh at the extensive biblical teaching on this theme, to endorse the conviction that followers of Jesus who are seeking God's kingdom will have different values and priorities from those around us, and to explore ways of living freely and joyfully within a culture that does not associate such notions with economics.

Among the questions we might ask are:

- In what ways do the prevailing economic system and culture dehumanize us and others?
- How can we become more fully human in our attitude towards and use of our homes, possessions and resources?
- What stories can we tell that will inspire us towards just, generous and creative ways of using our wealth as participants in God's mission?
- In what ways can the Christian community help to re-reflex us so that we respond to economic issues in counter-cultural ways?
- Should one in every seven sermons explore economic issues if we are to give due weight to the biblical emphasis, and what can we do to help each other apply what is preached?
- Can we write and sing more songs about economic justice, generosity and creativity?
- How can we transform 'the offering' in our churches into a more creative, missional, dynamic, radical element of our worship?
- What regular or occasional practices can we introduce into our gatherings to dethrone Mammon and nurture faithful discipleship in this area?
- How can we engage creatively in public debates about economic issues, offering not only unexpected theological perspectives but also practical examples of alternative ways of thinking and living?

If we are to make progress, though, we will need to confront a deep-seated reluctance to talk openly about economic discipleship within the Christian community. There are exceptions, especially in poorer communities, but in most churches this is a taboo subject once we move beyond generalities. Tom Sine of Mustard Seed Associates reports that many Christians were terrified by the thought of doing what a Mennonite church in Indiana did twice a year – bringing their budgets to the small group to which they belonged and asking this group to hold them accountable for what they had committed themselves to do with their finances for the next six months.[40]

Perhaps this is one reason why tithing is popular in some contexts: this individualistic mechanism requires no conversation about lifestyle and gives no opportunity to explore wider issues. In the very few New Testament references to this practice, tithing is associated with legalism and self-righteousness. It does little or nothing to address issues of economic injustice, build community, confront the culture of consumerism or dethrone Mammon.[41] Individualism and consumerism are a potent combination and powerfully obstruct progress towards faithful economic discipleship.

But the biblical writers were clearly not reluctant to discuss economic issues and a minority Christian community can choose to follow their lead. We can talk together about what we earn, how we earn it, what we spend, what we save, what we give, what we need, what we waste, how our culture tempts, how we resist this, on what basis we make financial choices, what it means to follow the One who came to bring good news to the poor, how we pursue economic justice for all, and what it means to be disciples in a consumerist society. And we need to set these conversations in a global context. We live in a very wealthy part of a world that is riddled with poverty. We are the beneficiaries of a deeply unjust global economy that was built on exploitation, is sustained by iniquitous trading practices, is damaging the planet, and is defended by violence or the threat of violence. We need communities of discernment and resistance to help us begin to find ways to live faithfully in such a context.

---

[40] Tom Sine, *Mustard Seed versus McWorld* (London: Monarch, 1999), pp. 288-9.

[41] See further Stuart Murray, *Beyond Tithing* (Carlisle: Paternoster, 2000).

And we can choose to experiment, to be creative, to be outrageously generous, to laugh together at ridiculous but alluring advertisements, to invest in transformational mission, to find a rhythm of fasting and feasting, to support each other in risky ventures, and to have godly fun with our finances. Our church café has an unusual loyalty card, the 'grub card': presenting this at the till means being charged an extra pound for the café to use to provide food for someone who cannot afford it. The Fremantle debt-clearance initiative mentioned in Chapter 3 is another example.

Idols cannot bear to be laughed at! In a society that takes economics very seriously, this may be one of the most effective ways of dethroning Mammon. In our words, deeds and priorities we can question, subvert and contradict the economic lunacy of our culture. We can challenge the 'myth of scarcity' that creates anxiety, restricts generosity and contradicts the abundance of God's good creation. There is enough for all if we practise just distribution.[42] We can unmask and ridicule the propaganda of the advertising industry, its unbelievable claims and its empty promises. And 'propaganda' is the appropriate word, given the origins of manipulative advertising techniques in the work of Edward Bernays, a propagandist in the First World War and nephew of Sigmund Freud, who is credited with transforming the way in which products were advertised and consumer desires were artificially stimulated.[43] We can resist the juggernaut of untrammelled consumerism and embrace the biblical virtue of contentment.[44]

However, we should be aware that this stance will align us with other subversive elements in society and will, if we were to throw the full weight of a vast minority behind it, bring down the wrath of those who are desperately trying to prop up a grossly unjust and unsustainable economic system. For, as Brian Walsh and Sylvia Keesmat warn, 'There is no word more offensive to a culture driven by unlimited economic growth than

[42] See further, William Cavanaugh, *Being Consumed: Economics and Christian Desire* (Grand Rapids: Eerdmans, 2008).

[43] See Larry Tye, *The Father of Spin: Edward L. Bernays and the Birth of Public Relations* (New York: Owl Books, 2002).

[44] See, for example, Phil. 4:11, 1 Tim. 6:8 and Heb. 13:5.

the word enough.'[45] Idols (and empires) do not appreciate being subverted!

At the very least, let's have some honest conversations about economic discipleship. In an individualistic culture, talking openly with each another about our finances may help us live imaginatively, responsibly and courageously – and not only in relation to our finances but in many other areas of discipleship. After all, Jesus did say: 'Where your treasure is, there your heart will be also.'[46] So maybe faithful, joyful, creative and counter-cultural discipleship in the area of economics can inspire us to similar practices in other areas of life.

---

[45] Brian Walsh and Sylvia Keesmat, *Colossians Re:mixed: Subverting the Empire* (Milton Keynes: Paternoster, 2005), p. 161.

[46] Matt. 6:21. He also told his disciples not to let their left hand know what their right hand is doing, warning them against making a show of their almsgiving (Matt. 6:3), but this is no bar on conversations about faithful economic discipleship.

5.

A Creative Minority

What Kind of Minority?

The Christian community in Britain and other Western societies will for the foreseeable future be a minority in a plural culture. This is now widely, if reluctantly, accepted, although some still cling to ways of measuring it that exaggerate its size and influence and others hope and pray that majority status might soon be restored. Relatively few are now unfamiliar with the terminology and implications of the transition from 'Christendom' to 'post-Christendom', although some struggle to see this as an opportunity for faithful discipleship and creative mission initiatives, arguing that some form of reconstituted Christendom is preferable to any alternatives.[1] But these are vain hopes and unpromising scenarios. It is time the conversation moved on, just as the Jewish exiles in Babylon needed to lay aside their illusory hopes of imminent deliverance, trust God's good purposes for them, settle down, and learn to live in their new surroundings. In this chapter we will return to Jeremiah's remarkable letter to the exiles as we reflect further on the vocation of the Christian community as a minority.

So the pertinent question now is not whether the Christian community is a minority or even what size this minority is. Our

---

[1] For example, a book that has made waves in North America but has had less traction in Europe, Peter Leithart, *Defending Constantine: The Twilight of an Empire and the Dawn of Christendom* (Downers Grove: IVP, 2010). A British example is Michael Bochenski, *Transforming Faith Communities* (Eugene, OR: Wipf & Stock, 2013), a comparative study of Anabaptism and liberation theology that advocates a blend of congregationalism and a renewed Christendom.

working assumption, which might be too low or too high, has been roughly 10 per cent of the population in Britain. This is a 'vast minority' with extensive resources and the capacity to exercise great influence. There are certainly things we can no longer do – and things we should never have done when we were a majority – but there are also things we can do better and things we have not done before.

But what kind of minority will we be? There are many possibilities. We could be a frightened, despondent and beleaguered minority preoccupied with institutional survival and increasingly disconnected from the rest of society. We could be a fragmented and fractious minority, arguing over internal issues, drawing lines in the sand to exclude others and exhausting ourselves with infighting. We could be a militant and belligerent minority, protesting vociferously whenever our sensibilities are offended or our interests are threatened. We could be a compliant and anodyne minority, watering down our distinctive truth claims, making sure we do not give offence, and allowing ourselves to be co-opted in return for recognition and appreciation. These are deeply unattractive futures, but they are present realities in some sections of the Christian community. We urgently need a more compelling vision.

What if we embraced the opportunity to be a 'creative minority'? What if we agreed with Richard Koenig, who wrote: 'The role of a creative minority might possibly be that form of pilgrimage to which God is calling his church'?[2]

Many activists and writers have recognized the huge potential of minorities. Essayist and poet Ralph Waldo Emerson insisted: 'The truth, the hope of any time, must always be sought in minorities.' Eugene Victor Debs, an early socialist and pioneering union leader, concluded: 'When great changes occur in history, when great principles are involved, as a rule the majority are wrong. The minority are right.' Lawyer Harlan Stone declared: 'Democracy cannot survive without the guidance of a creative minority.' Emma Goldman, renowned (and vilified) anarchist and feminist, wrote: 'Every effort for progress, for enlightenment, for science, for religious, political, and economic liberty, emanates from the

---

[2] Richard Koenig, *A Creative Minority: The Church in a New Age* (Minneapolis: Augsburg, 1971), p. 34.

minority, and not from the mass.' And civil rights activist Martin Luther King Jr reflected: 'Almost always, the creative dedicated minority has made the world better.' Why does a minority have such creative potential? German rabbi and scholar Leo Baeck explains: 'A minority is always compelled to think. That is the blessing of being in the minority.'

Minorities can do things that majorities either cannot or will not. Arne Rasmusson, professor of systematic theology at the University of Gothenburg, explains that they can 'carry ideas and practices that at the moment seem unrealistic, and therefore are not an option for the power at hand, but that at a later time may become credible. A minority can do this because they do not primarily evaluate their faith and practice according to public opinion or in terms of short reign effectiveness.'[3] Minorities may be less concerned about their reputation, social standing, numerical strength and institutional stability. They are not hamstrung by the need to be successful or maintain control. They have less invested in the status quo, are prepared to question what most regard as 'common sense' and so can imagine new possibilities and pioneer new initiatives. They notice what majorities ignore or fail to recognize. They can experiment and take risks majorities regard as foolhardy. They can bring fresh thinking to perennial and contemporary issues. Minorities can be creative.

A Creative Minority

The term 'creative minority' has been used by two very influential religious leaders in recent years. In 2004, Cardinal Joseph Ratzinger, later to become Pope Benedict XVI, drew on the writings of the historian Arnold Toynbee who designated creative minorities 'history's great problem solvers'. Ratzinger suggested, in a lecture on the Christian roots of Europe, that 'Christian believers should look upon themselves as just such a creative minority, and help Europe to reclaim what is best in its heritage and to therefore place itself at the service of all humankind'. This is an extraordinary proposal from someone who would shortly become the

---

[3] Arne Rasmusson, *The Church as Polis* (Lund: Lund University Press, 1994), p. 373.

spiritual head of a global Christian community that has long been accustomed to being and behaving as a dominant majority. It represents official acknowledgement of minority status, at least in Europe, and encourages this minority community to choose a creative future.

In 2013, 'creative minority' was the main theme of Rabbi Jonathan Sacks' Erasmus Lecture. He noted with great interest Cardinal Ratzinger's use of the term and traced the notion of a creative minority back to Jeremiah's counsel to the exiles in Babylon. He suggested that the experience of the Jewish community over the centuries might hold clues for how religious communities, especially Jews and Christians, might conduct themselves in a secular Europe. This lecture, which illustrates the claim made in an earlier chapter that a minority Christian community might learn from the Jewish experience, contains much wisdom and is worth reading in full.[4]

Sacks recognized, as we have done above, that there are other less creative ways a minority can respond to their diminished status:

> First, it can accommodate to secularization: the way of religious liberalism. Second, it can resist it, sometimes violently, as religiously extremist groups are doing in many parts of the world today. Third, it can withdraw into protected enclaves, much as we see happening in certain groups within Orthodox Judaism. This is a powerful strategy, and it has strengthened Jewish Orthodoxy immensely, but at the price of segregation from – and thus loss of influence on – the world outside.

But he advocated the alternative and more attractive approach commended to the Jewish exiles in Babylon. 'What Jeremiah was saying was that it is possible to survive in exile with your identity intact, your appetite for life undiminished, while contributing to the wider society and praying to God on its behalf. Jeremiah was introducing into history a highly consequential idea: the idea of a creative minority.'

Setting out various ways in which the minority Jewish community was creative in Babylon and in subsequent centuries, he concluded:

---

[4] A transcript of this lecture can be found at http://www.rabbisacks.org/creative-minorities-transcript-rabbi-sacks-erasmus-lecture.

So you can be a minority, living in a country whose religion, culture, and legal system are not your own, and yet sustain your identity, live your faith, and contribute to the common good, exactly as Jeremiah said. It isn't easy. It demands a complex finessing of identities. It involves a willingness to live in a state of cognitive dissonance. It isn't for the fainthearted. But it is creative.

Creativity and Resistance

Celebrating the creative potential of a minority community, however, may be easier than wrestling with the issues involved in moving from majority to minority status. If the Christian community is to seize the opportunities of being a creative minority, we must whole-heartedly embrace this new reality and disavow many past assumptions and practices. We have already considered some of the temptations an ex-majority community needs to resist.[5] Re-imagining ourselves as a creative minority is a paradigm shift and will not be accomplished overnight or without resistance.

Some of this resistance will come from the Christian community itself as it struggles to move beyond innate conservatism, risk aversion and fear of the unknown. We will need to embrace a 'theology of risk' if the Christian community is to be a conducive place to be creative and a loving refuge for those who encounter disappointment. We will need to be both gracious and rigorous as we assess changes and evaluate experimental initiatives. We will need to be wary of defining 'success' in ways that suited the old paradigm but are inappropriate for the new paradigm. Short-lived experiments, apparent dead ends and limited returns on the investment of people and funds may not be failures but opportunities for discovery, reflection and further courageous ventures. We will need both to be persistent and patient with initiatives that show promise but are slow to mature, and also willing to bring ventures to an end without regarding them or those who have invested much in them as failures.

Some of the resistance will come from outside the Christian community. Long accustomed to regarding the Christian

---

[5] See Chapter 3.

community as reactionary, tradition-bound, predictable and moribund, responses to creative initiatives will understandably be guarded and suspicious. Motives will be questioned and hidden agendas sought. Failures will be highlighted and successes ignored or explained away. Inconsistencies and inadequacies will be seized upon and critique will be harsh. We will do well to be slow to take offence or react badly to criticism. Our track record as a majority community is very mixed and we cannot expect this legacy to be discounted or our changed attitudes and activities as a minority community to be welcomed without demur. Persistence, grace and patience will be the watchwords here too.

It is in this spirit, then, that we reflect on four popular and heralded initiatives that represent attempts to renew the Christian community and enhance its impact in a changing society.

Back to Church Sunday

Over recent years several denominations have organized an annual 'Back to Church' Sunday, promoted as an opportunity for people with previous experience of church to return and make a fresh start. Congregations have been encouraged to make a determined effort to be friendly, welcoming and accessible on this occasion. Attractive literature has been distributed widely and members of the congregation have invited friends and neighbours. Experience has varied, but there have been enough encouraging reports for this initiative to continue, with as many as thirty thousand churches expected to participate in 2014. An extensive website provides ideas and resources.[6]

There is much to commend in this initiative. It indicates recognition of the increased cultural distance between most congregations and wider society. It represents a more proactive stance that no longer assumes congregations simply arrange services and expect people to attend. If it results in congregations becoming warmer, more engaging, better contextualized and more creative (and not just once a year), and if people reconnect with the Christian community and with God, these are excellent outcomes.

[6] See http://backtochurch.com/.

However, this initiative is predicated on the availability of significant numbers of people with previous church connections who are open to an invitation to return. This constituency exists but is primarily located in neighbourhoods in which church attendance has been quite normal and in the higher age ranges. Those who were children in middle-class neighbourhoods in the 1950s may be susceptible to this approach, but the dramatic decline in church and Sunday-school attendance in the 1960s means that many of those who are younger have no memories of church. And in many inner-city neighbourhoods there are few people with former church links.[7]

The terminology also implies that church attendance is normal and non-attendance is unusual, or even shameful. Graham Cray comments: 'Whole strategies of evangelism have been based on a residual guilt about not going to church.'[8] John and Olive Drane report:

> We came across a group of churches (in Scotland) that decided to address the problem of a long-term decline in membership and attendance by offering the population of its area what was described as an 'amnesty' on church membership, whereby people who had allowed their membership to 'lapse' could return on a no-questions-asked sort of basis. Such an offer would only make sense on the assumption that Christendom is still alive and well, that the church has a right to expect loyalty from the wider population, and that if we Christians can no longer engage effectively with other people, that is not our problem, but theirs.[9]

And Paul Roberts writes:

> The Constantinian assumptions underlying such 'shop window' worship should be obvious. Christian worship is seen as a *socially*

---

7   See further Roger Standing, *Re-Emerging Church: Strategies for Reaching a Returning Generation* (Oxford: Bible Reading Fellowship, 2008).
8   Graham Cray, *Youth Congregations and the Emerging Church* (Nottingham: Grove, 2002), p. 9.
9   John and Olive Drane, 'Breaking into Dynamic Ways of being Church', in *Breaking New Ground* (material prepared for the First Scottish Ecumenical Assembly, 2001).

normal activity, in a state where Christian social hegemony is also normal. The role of the 'unchurched' in seeker-friendly and 'back-to-church' approaches is that of the deviant, rather than the norm. In these missiologies that use worship as a point of attraction, adapted liturgies are being used as a therapy for socio-religious deviance. In post-Christendom, however, *worship itself is a form of social deviance.*[10]

This initiative may continue with varying levels of effectiveness for several years yet until its designated constituency disappears, but critics are concerned that it may be a distraction from the missional thinking a minority community needs. It prioritizes those often referred to as the 'de-churched' or 'semi-churched' (problematic terms that also imply the normality of being 'churched' and a deficiency in those who are not), but this is a shrinking constituency. It makes minor adjustments to church life, or at least to some public events, but continues to operate in attractional mode. And it has little or nothing to offer to neighbourhoods in which church attendance has been unusual for generations.

Alpha

The Alpha course, developed and brilliantly marketed by Holy Trinity, Brompton, has been for the past twenty-five years the highest profile of several evangelism/discipleship courses that have become the mainstay of many congregations.[11] These courses represent a decisive shift from previous models of evangelism. Their distinctive features are opportunities for conversation and discussion following a presentation, rather than listening passively; eating together in a relaxed environment; and recognition that participants may consider what they have heard for several weeks before making any commitment. Although courses are normally hosted in church buildings, they have taken place in community centres, restaurants, hotels and other more neutral venues, and the Alpha course has been used in many prisons.

There is much to celebrate in these developments. This approach is endorsed by research over the past three decades into

---

[10] Paul Roberts, in *The Gospel after Christendom* (ed. Ryan Bolger; Grand Rapids: Baker, 2012), p. 182 (italics his).

[11] See http://www.alpha.org.

how people actually come to faith in Jesus Christ. Friendship, time to consider and unpressured conversations are all important. Although still mainly attractional in ethos, the use of other venues reflects greater sensitivity to a changed cultural context and recognition that church buildings are not necessarily conducive to those not already members of a minority Christian community. And there are numerous stories of participants in these courses who have come to faith in Christ and whose lives have been transformed (although the story of a man who became an atheist on an Alpha course was for some reason less well reported!).

However, these courses have serious limitations and may not assist the Christian community that much in the transition to minority status. Critics have expressed various concerns: most of the courses are quite cerebral, despite an emphasis in some on the work of the Holy Spirit, presenting a propositional approach to Christian faith; many assume familiarity with concepts and terms that are unknown to many outside the Christian community; most do not start far enough back on the journey towards faith and move too quickly; and participants often report that the discussions are unduly proscribed.[12] A group led by a friend of mine asked him at the end of the course: 'Now we've discussed the questions you wanted us to, can we move on to the questions we want to ask?' The reluctance of the Alpha organization to engage in careful research into who participates also means that it is impossible to know how many are already involved in the churches that run them, but anecdotal evidence suggests that only a minority are actually from beyond the Christian community. The Alpha course, like Back to Church Sunday, perpetuates an attractional approach to evangelism that expects people to come to church-organized events rather than an incarnational approach of going to them where they are. If the understanding of church members is enhanced and their faith renewed, and others on the fringe of church life are drawn into the community and to faith in Christ, these are, of course, positive outcomes. But other approaches may be required for a minority community to communicate effectively with most people in contemporary culture.

[12] See further Andrew Brookes, ed., *The Alpha Phenomenon* (London: CTBI, 2007). However, other courses (such as Start, Essence and Emmaus) do represent attempts to address some of these issues.

There are other concerns. There are restrictions placed on those who use the Alpha resources, limiting their freedom to adapt these to local situations. Whatever the justifications for this, a more contextualized approach is needed in the diverse culture in which a minority Christian community now bears witness. The theological content of the Alpha course is traditional (but not conservative enough for some who have developed other courses) and betrays no hint of creativity, critical engagement with the impact of majority status on theological perspectives, or openness to fresh ways of thinking. And bolting courses of this kind onto existing churches without taking into account the differences in ethos and style causes difficulties and does not, as many have discovered, result in the kind of ecclesial renewal that is required.

Fresh Expressions

Ecclesial renewal and missional impact are at the heart of 'fresh expressions of church', so it might be helpful to devote a rather longer section to assessing this initiative, though it is too early to attempt more than a provisional assessment. It was only in 2004 that the term was coined and gained acceptance as a more congenial term to describe a range of experimental initiatives that had previously been labelled more challengingly 'new ways of being church' or 'emerging churches'. The endorsement given to these initiatives by Rowan Williams, then archbishop of Canterbury, the huge popularity of the *Mission-Shaped Church* report,[13] and the generous funding of the Fresh Expressions team resulted in the rapid proliferation of 'fresh expressions of church', initially in Anglican circles, then among Methodists, and then more broadly as most of the main denominations either became formal partners or set up similar initiatives. And the pace has increased significantly since 2010.

It will, therefore, be some years yet before it is clear what lasting impact these initiatives have had and to what extent they are helping the Christian community adjust to its minority status and changed role within society. Rather than offering any definitive assessment at this stage, then, it might be more helpful to present two very different perspectives that highlight some of the

[13] *Mission-Shaped Church* (London: Church House, 2004).

issues that will need to be addressed as these 'fresh expressions of church' mature and find their place within the wider Christian community.

Advocates of 'fresh expressions of church' can point to some very impressive outcomes, as the 2014 progress report makes clear.[14] These include:

- Thousands of examples across Britain and, more recently, in other nations as news of these initiatives has inspired churches elsewhere.
- Large numbers of church members becoming more missionally involved in their local communities.
- Significant numbers of former church members reconnecting with the churches and finding their faith rekindled.
- Equally significant numbers of people with no previous church involvement coming to faith in Jesus Christ and joining the Christian community.
- The development of extensive resources, learning communities, training courses and opportunities to share stories and develop expertise.
- Greater sensitivity to contextual factors in developing mission strategies, encouraging churches to explore ways to incarnate the gospel effectively in their communities.[15]
- Heightened understanding of the dynamics of forming new Christian communities, including the importance of careful research and preparation, and experience in team building.

What is much less clear is the long-term ecclesial status and prospects of these initiatives. It is encouraging to hear advocates of 'fresh expressions of church' insisting that these are not 'church-lite' adjuncts to 'proper' church or in any way secondary to inherited expressions of church – and urging everyone to call them

[14] http://www.freshexpressions.org.uk/news/anglicanresearch. This report identified 518 examples in only 10 dioceses and only investigated Anglican initiatives. Extrapolating this figure suggests over 2,000 Anglican initiatives in England alone.

[15] The title of Michael Moynagh's text book emphasizes this aspect of fresh expressions: *Church for Every Context: An Introduction to Theology and Practice* (London: SCM Press, 2013).

'fresh expressions *of church*', rather than 'fresh expressions'. But how will these thousands of new 'ecclesial communities' (as one advocate prefers to call them) relate to inherited denominational structures as the years go by? There seem to be three main options: to become churches on an equal footing with other churches in their denomination; to be absorbed back into the congregations from which they emerged; or to remain linked to existing congregations or other ecclesial bodies without attaining full ecclesial status.

There are advantages and drawbacks in each of these scenarios. Becoming established and recognized as fully-fledged churches indicates acceptance that these are authentic expressions of Christian community and that they are expected to be sustainable. The danger, however, is that they lose their missional edge and become encumbered by institutional expectations and responsibilities. Being absorbed back into the congregations that supported them might seem to indicate that they were never expected to be more than short-term experiments and that the main purpose was actually to draw people into 'proper' church, but some fresh expressions are unlikely ever to become sustainable and, if they bring fresh missional dynamism into the congregation, this might be a very positive outcome. Remaining linked to a congregation or other ecclesial body (such as a Methodist circuit) risks consigning the fresh expression to an ecclesial twilight zone, but if relationships are healthy this might enable it to maintain its missional focus while drawing on the resources of the inherited church.

Ten years from now, then, we might look back at the 'fresh expressions' initiative as a timely and effective strategy that enabled the Christian community to wrestle with the complexities of a changing and diverse culture, explore creative and contextual approaches to mission and church, slow the apparently inexorable decline and even stimulate some growth in numbers and influence. We might conclude that this was just the kind of initiative of which Jeremiah would have approved when he encouraged the Jewish exiles to take courage, build houses, plant vineyards, bless their neighbours and patiently rebuild in Babylon.[16]

Critics are not persuaded that this initiative is as significant as its advocates suggest and some are concerned that it might be a

---

[16] Jer. 29:5–7. See further in Chapter 3.

distraction from addressing the deeper issues involved in learning to be a faithful minority community. Jeremiah warned, after all, about the danger of looking for a quick and painless escape from exile.[17] There were important lessons for the Jewish community to learn in Babylon and there were no short cuts. It would take time for them to review their history and disavow some aspects of this. It would take time for them to work through the profound theological challenge presented by exile and to learn to read their Scriptures in fresh ways. It would take time to learn to love their enemies and discover the scope and depth of God's *shalom*.

Can 'fresh expressions of church' grapple with these deeper issues? Are they willing to do so? Are they even aware of these issues? Not according to a leading proponent of 'fresh expressions' in a recent conversation. Or are they attempts to refresh a weary institution and prolong denominational survival without engaging in the more demanding but crucial task of theological, missional and ecclesial reformation? Are they imparting a false sense of security?

Some of the concerns raised in the early days have been addressed. No longer can anyone register as a 'fresh expression of church' without some level of scrutiny, thus precluding the frequently mocked examples that once appeared on the Fresh Expressions website. There is now a much tighter definition of what constitutes a 'fresh expression'. There has also been much more missiological reflection, the sharing of best practice and the development of an impressive range of training courses and resources. And recent research indicates, despite some methodological weaknesses that warn us to treat its findings with caution, that many 'fresh expressions' are connecting with people beyond the reach of inherited churches.

But concerns remain. The *Mission-Shaped Church* report described a range of initiatives that might previously have been subsumed under the rubric of 'church planting' but were in many ways different from traditional forms of church planting. Dubbing these 'fresh expressions of church', the report's authors chose to avoid the term 'emerging church' that was also gaining currency at that time. Furthermore, the report quoted with approval a phrase used by Rowan Williams before he became archbishop of Canterbury –

[17] Jer. 29:8–14.

'mixed economy' – and this phrase has been repeated ad nauseam. The terminology was politically acute and typically Anglican, affirming a 'both/and' rather than 'either/or' approach. These 'fresh expressions' were not to be perceived as threats to the status quo but as initiatives alongside inherited forms of church. Undoubtedly, this approach has enabled 'fresh expressions' to proliferate and find acceptance across the Anglican communion and in several other denominations. But at what cost?

It was not just that the phrase 'mixed economy' became somewhat tainted once the economic crisis broke a few years later ('mixed ecology' was proposed as an alternative). These phrases conveyed, wittingly or not, the implication that the institution did not need to consider radical changes or ask searching questions about its role in a social context in which it was no longer a majority. And the role of the Fresh Expressions team has also prompted concerns. Although ostensibly offering support, training and encouragement, have they in effect domesticated and franchised 'fresh expressions of church'? How creative and contextual are these initiatives if several hundred in diverse communities have adopted the same model? To what extent has an opportunity for exploration and experimentation been subjected to institutional control? And some have expressed concern about the pressure on other denominations to join an Anglican initiative, detecting the kind of ecumenical imperialism that is no longer appropriate for any denomination in a minority community.

What was lost when the choice was made to avoid the more provocative but more liberating term 'emerging church'? There are strengths and weaknesses with this term – and with the diverse initiatives that have embraced it or to which this label has been attached. But in many 'emerging churches' conversations were taking place at a much deeper theological level and many of the crucial hermeneutical, ethical and attitudinal issues were being addressed. Some of these conversations were worrying to inherited churches, raising uncomfortable issues and asking awkward questions. And some of those involved were less susceptible to institutional control. Not all were as ostensibly missional as initiatives that would soon be termed 'fresh expressions of church', nor did they seem to offer such good prospects for numerical growth. There were understandable reasons for avoiding this terminology and sidelining these initiatives. But we might conclude that there have been losses as well as gains.

How can we decide which of these perspectives offers a more accurate assessment of 'fresh expressions of church'? It may simply be too early to make this kind of judgement. We could adopt the Gamaliel 'wait and see' stance.[18] Or we could adopt a mediating position in which we acknowledge the limitations of this initiative but celebrate its accomplishments. Perhaps what has happened over the past fifteen years or so is the first wave and maybe the next wave will carry us into deeper water.

Festivals

Christian festivals and Bible weeks have a much longer history than the three initiatives we have considered so far, although they seem to have proliferated in recent years. Greenbelt and Spring Harvest are perhaps the best known and best attended, but there are numerous others catering for a range of theological tastes and interests. Some seem designed to stretch those who attend, challenge familiar notions and encourage fresh perspectives. Others seem more designed to reinforce and buttress the views participants already hold. Not all have managed to attract enough participants to survive – another indication of too many organizations and ventures competing for a share of a diminishing constituency – and others are likely to go under in the near future.

What do these events contribute as the Christian community transitions to minority status? Many of those who attend these festivals are members of small congregations, some of which are ageing and declining. Worshipping, learning and interacting with hundreds or thousands of others can be hugely encouraging and a reminder that they belong to a 'vast minority' that still has the capacity to achieve much. These events can broaden perspectives, renew vision and energy, forge lasting friendships and partnerships, and stimulate fresh initiatives in local contexts all over the country. They may be of increasing importance to a minority community if we are to resist parochialism, counter isolation and discouragement, and explore creative ways of deploying our resources.

---

[18] See Acts 5:34–9.

But the tone of these festivals needs to reflect the reality of a minority community if they are to be authentic rather than hollow. Most are understandably celebratory and upbeat, but this needs to be tempered with other moods if they are not to become escapist and disconnected from the lived experience of participants throughout the rest of the year. Several years ago I was invited to a consultation in advance of a Spring Harvest event, at which the organizers outlined the programme and welcomed comments. The 'post-Christendom' theme would be explored through studies in the book of Daniel and in many other ways – an opportunity to reflect on the implications of becoming a minority community in a changing culture. And the title of the event was taken from Psalm 137 in which disorientated exiles ask how they can sing the Lord's song in a strange land. However, some of us were disturbed to learn that the title was 'Sing the Lord's Song!' with an exclamation mark rather than a question mark. After some discussion the organizers took the point and suggested that the exclamation mark could be removed, but introducing a question mark was a step too far. We probed further, asking whether the event could include some songs of lament as well as songs of joyful celebration and triumph. This caused some consternation, partly because the organizers were not convinced the musicians knew any such songs, and partly because they wanted the event to be uncompromisingly joyful and celebratory – whatever the subject.

Is it churlish to propose two cheers, rather than three, for these initiatives? They represent a remarkable investment of time, money, energy, personnel and creativity. Without them the Christian community would be less well resourced, less well interconnected and less well prepared for life as a minority community. They have been the means by which thousands of people have heard the gospel, come to faith in Christ or renewed their commitment to him. Lives have been transformed. New churches have been planted and older churches have been renewed and revitalized. And they have restored confidence in the gospel and revived hope that the Christian community can experience growth in the midst of decline. Withholding the third cheer is an expression of concern that these ventures do not lull us into a false sense of security. They have placed great demands on those directly involved, and many have required the permission, support and endorsement of denominational and congregational leaders. But most have not seriously questioned institutional priorities, provoked debate about the role of the Christian community within a changing culture or inspired creative theological reflection.

Creativity and Theology

The conjunction of creativity and theology can be worrying. Creativity is all very well in the context of fresh expressions of church and experimental mission ventures, but we can become resistant, or at least rather nervous, when creative approaches to theology, ethics and biblical interpretation are advocated. Concerns are expressed about 'watering down the gospel' and being 'conformed to the world'. Traditional formulations of doctrine, settled ethical positions and standard interpretations of biblical teaching are regarded as non-negotiable. Pioneers are warned about the danger of slipping into heresy, and some feel under pressure to declare their theological orthodoxy if they are to retain support. Those who dare to question long-held and precious convictions can find they have stirred up a hornet's nest. Recent controversies in the evangelical section of the Christian community around ways of understanding the atonement and ethical/pastoral perspectives on homosexuality amply demonstrate this.

And these are legitimate concerns. One of the temptations facing a minority community is to seek acceptance by abandoning its distinctive convictions, values and practices and becoming accommodated to the surrounding culture. Revising its stance on ethical issues if this is out of kilter with contemporary sensibilities can be presented as 'progressive' and legitimated on the basis of a fresh interpretation of the biblical material, as can adjusting doctrinal convictions that are uncongenial or offensive to our contemporaries. And advocates of these revisions and adjustments may reject any suggestion that they are unduly influenced by public opinion. But if all the revisions and adjustments diminish the particularity and nonconformity of the minority community and none present fresh challenges to the surrounding culture, critics are understandably unconvinced.

However, an ex-majority community in a changing culture does have an opportunity to revisit and review what it believes and to investigate the influence of its previous majority status on its theology, ethics and biblical interpretation. Maybe earlier generations were concerned to accommodate their beliefs and practices to their culture and were unduly influenced by these. Perhaps majority status predisposed them to interpret the Bible and formulate doctrines in certain ways and to adopt ethical positions that owed as much to their context and interests as to biblical teaching. A minority community may see things to which a majority community is blind. Minority Christian communities in the past have frequently recovered dimensions of the Christian faith and discipleship practices that had been obscured or marginalized – and these were very often more radical rather than more culturally accommodating. Theological creativity today might encourage a minority Christian community in a similar direction.

Doing theology with new conversation partners

Living in Babylon threw up new theological and ethical issues for the Jewish exiles to ponder and discuss. Or, at least, their changed context invited them to think afresh about perennial issues and resulted in them revisiting and re-appropriating their Scriptures. We sampled some of these issues and responses in Chapter 2. Not only were they required to engage with a very different political, social, cultural and economic context; they also had new conversation partners with whom to debate these issues.

For hundreds of years, European theologians have operated within a dominant community. In the early church, theologians and apologists from a minority Christian community debated in person and in their writings with Jews, pagan philosophers, priests of popular oriental cults and others. Some of the leading theologians were catechists, interacting with people from diverse backgrounds interested in the Christian faith. They were engaged on the front line of mission and discipleship. Theology and ethics were forged in this crucible. Theologians in Asia throughout the centuries also had various conversation partners – Zoroastrians, Hindus, Buddhists, Muslims and others. But European theology in the Christendom era developed within an exclusive theological guild that was largely unaware of or uninterested in other perspectives. Eventually, the challenge of secularists and atheists attracted the attention of apologists, but most theologians have continued to debate with other theologians, addressing topics of interest within the academy.

One of the consequences of this is a profound disconnect between the academy and the local congregation, to the detriment of both. Another is the marginalizing of theological insights from other parts of the global Christian community. International symposia and conferences, journals and books, and the immense resources available via the internet have made these easily accessible, but non-Western theologies continue to be perceived as 'contextual', with Western theology regarded as normative. 'Black theology', for example, is welcomed as an interesting perspective, but European theologians tend to bristle if their discipline is referred to as 'White theology'. Most Western theological colleges include non-Western books only in the bibliographies of specialist modules. But the demise of Christendom, the growth of the Christian community in Africa and Asia and the expansion of non-European churches within Europe mean that a truly global theological conversation is crucial. And Western theologians, as members of what is now a minority branch of the global Christian community, might look to their colleagues elsewhere increasingly to set the agenda and take the lead. The insights of theologians in contexts where the Christian community has long been a minority will offer much to the Christian community in Western societies as we adjust to minority status. Their contributions can also help us differentiate between biblical and cultural perspectives.[19]

But it is not only Christian theologians from other cultures and contexts that we need as our conversation partners. In a plural culture such as we have not experienced in Europe since the

[19] Timothy Tennent identifies five trends in what he appropriately calls Majority World theology: a conservative view of Scripture, conservative ethics, sensitivity to social justice, an ability to articulate the uniqueness of the gospel in the context of religious pluralism, and greater attunement to corporate dimensions of the gospel. See Timothy Tennent, *Theology in the Context of World Christianity* (Grand Rapids: Zondervan, 2007), pp. 14–15. Not all of these perspectives will be attractive to many Western theologians.

early centuries, our conversation partners must include Muslims, Hindus, Sikhs, Buddhists, Jews, atheists, neo-pagans, animists and others. Their assumptions, convictions, questions and resources have the capacity to challenge, enrich and reshape our theological discussions. What can we learn from the Jewish community about Sabbath practice, for example, or from Muslims about usury (about which the Old Testament says much but the church says little), or from neo-pagans and animists about our relationship with our environment?

This will require courage, humility and a paradigm shift. As Timothy Tennent, theologian and president of Asbury Theological Seminary, comments, 'The basic problem is that Western systematic theologies are still written with a Christendom mind-set, assuming the absence of rival theistic claims as well as rival sacred texts. They tend to be overly preoccupied with philosophical objections to the Christian message, rather than with religious objections based on sacred texts or major social traditions that contradict the claims of Scripture.'[20] Christopher Sinkinson of Moorlands College concurs: 'Christian theology has failed to deal adequately with the fact that we live in a world of myriad religious traditions . . . If theology is to be relevant in the future it must have serious engagement not only with secular atheism but also with alternative religious traditions.'[21]

Doing theology in a multi-faith context does not mean compromising or downplaying our Christian convictions, but it does mean attentiveness to our new conversation partners and openness to fresh insights and different ways of thinking about old questions. An academic example is the initiative known as A Common Word, in which Muslim scholars invited Christian scholars to an ongoing theological conversation based on mutual respect and an exploration of the sacred texts of each community.[22] Another example at a local community level is the House of One in Berlin, a building housing a synagogue, church and mosque under one roof, an initiative of the Protestant pastor, Gregor Hohberg. Each community will have its own space and retain its distinctive convictions

---

[20] Tennent, *Theology in the Context of World Christianity*, p. 257.

[21] In Tony Gray and Christopher Sinkinson, eds, *Reconstructing Theology* (Carlisle: Paternoster, 2000), p. 155.

[22] See http://www.acommonword.com.

and practices. Hohberg explains: 'We want to use these rooms for our own traditions and prayers. And together we want to use the room in the middle for dialogue and discussion and also for people without faith.'[23]

Jonathan Sacks calls for something similar involving the Christian and Jewish communities, now that the Christian community is a minority alongside other minorities: 'The time has come for a new meeting of Christians and Jews, based simply on the fact that a church that sees itself as a creative minority in the Jeremiah sense has made space for the existence of Jews and Judaism in a way that was not fully articulated before.'[24] Minority status offers opportunities as well as imposing limitations. Doing theology as a minority community in conversation with others will be challenging, but it holds all kinds of creative possibilities.

Reading the Bible from the margins

It is now widely acknowledged that biblical interpretation is influenced by the context within which it takes place and the social, economic and cultural location of the interpreter. Biblical interpretation during the era when the church was a powerful and wealthy political institution, presiding over a largely nominal Christian society, reflected this context. Interpreters tended to read the Bible in socially conservative ways that did not challenge a supposedly Christian status quo, emphasizing obedience to the authorities, undergirding the prevailing economic system, and endorsing sacral, patriarchal and hierarchical governance.

There were, of course, dissenting voices who drew attention to texts and themes in the Bible that seemed to point in very different directions. Despite the efforts of the authorities to keep the Bible out of the hands of those who might interpret it in unorthodox and subversive ways, and their intolerance of movements that emerged from these fresh encounters with Scripture, the interpretive consensus was persistently challenged by those who were captivated by the Bible's radical, prophetic, missional and eschatological message. These alternative readings, together with

---

[23] See further http://www.bbc.co.uk/news/magazine-27872551.

[24] http://www.rabbisacks.org/creative-minorities-transcript-rabbi-sacks-erasmus-lecture.

insights from the global church in which many interpreters are not located in majority Christian communities, may be resources on which a minority Christian community can draw as we review standard interpretations and learn to read the Bible from the margins rather than the centre. This process has been underway for some time in academic circles but has yet to impact most of the Christian community.[25]

Some examples from the gospels will help to illustrate this change of perspective. Many of the parables Jesus told feature authority figures – kings, judges, wealthy farmers, noblemen, vineyard owners, slave masters – and traditional interpretations frequently assume that they represent God. But this identification is problematic in many cases, not least because of the way some of them behave, and leads to applications that are economically, politically and socially uninteresting. A minority community, reading the Parable of the Pounds (in Luke 19:11–27) from the margins, might dissent from the traditional interpretation which honours those servants who kowtow to their absent master's expectations and behave like energetic capitalists. They might instead regard the servant who buried his pound in the ground as the hero for refusing to participate in the rapacious economic practices of his vindictive master. Support for this deviant reading can be found in the surrounding text as Jesus celebrates the salvation of Zacchaeus, who renounces economic injustice and gives generously to those he has cheated, and in the expulsion from the temple courts of those who were polluting it with their economic activities.

Economic issues also feature in the story of the rich young ruler in the previous chapter (Luke 18:18–25). Preachers operating with standard interpretations of this passage understandably identify members of their congregations with the rich man (Western Christians are, after all, very wealthy in global terms) and encourage us

---

[25] Among many helpful resources, see for example: Walter Wink, *Engaging the Powers* (Minneapolis: Fortress Press, 1992); Lloyd Pietersen, *Reading the Bible after Christendom* (Milton Keynes: Paternoster, 2011); Warren Carter, *Matthew and the Margins* (Maryknoll: Orbis, 2005); Kenneth Bailey, *Jesus through Middle Eastern Eyes* (London: SPCK, 2008); and Ched Myers, *Binding the Strong Man* (Maryknoll: Orbis, 2008).

to lay aside whatever hinders us from whole-hearted discipleship. Some courageous preachers will go beyond this generic application and insist that the passage is about our economic priorities. But very rarely do these sermons even mention the other character in the story. What other character? I have invited many groups to read the passage again, looking for anyone else except Jesus and the rich young ruler. Most continue to look puzzled. But Jesus invites the rich young to distribute his money *to the poor.* This story is not just about a rich man's excessive wealth and the impact on his spiritual life, but about redistribution to those who do not have enough. Those who are poor and read this passage from the margins notice this and wonder when wealthy followers of Jesus will obey his teaching. Those who are wealthy and read from the centre do not even see the poor person in the story.

Matthew 13 contains several parables in which Jesus says, 'The kingdom of heaven is like . . .' The Parable of the Weeds (vv. 24–30) is one of two that Jesus explains to his disciples (in vv. 37–43). Despite this, two quite different interpretations have competed for acceptance over the years. The mainstream interpretation has been to use this parable to justify the existence of a 'mixed' church and to resist any suggestion that distinctions should be made between good seed and weeds until the return of Christ. This suited a largely nominal Christian culture in which the churches often had low moral standards. But this interpretation ignored two vital features of the parable and Jesus' own explanation. This is a parable of the kingdom, not of the church, and the field in which good seed and weeds are mixed is not the church but the world. Dissenters through the centuries have insisted that 'church' and 'world' are different categories (despite the tendency of a dominant Christian community to conflate them and to identify the institutional church with the kingdom of God) and have pursued an alternative vision of a disciplined and faithful church, however small a minority this is within society.

The same chapter contains the brief Parable of the Mustard Seed (vv. 31–32), which interpreters in majority Christian contexts have frequently used to celebrate the remarkable growth of the church from tiny beginnings and its impressive size. They have painted a word picture of a majestic tree like an oak or a cedar of Lebanon. But mustard seeds do not grow into trees but, as Jesus actually says, into large shrubs. Rather than growing upwards, they spread outwards and dig their roots in, making them resilient to being uprooted. And this again is not a parable of the church but of the kingdom of heaven. As a minority community reads this parable from the margins, maybe it will realize that its vocation is not cultural domination but putting down deep roots, developing resilience and getting involved in all kinds of down-to-earth ministry.

In an earlier chapter I mentioned my involvement in the Crucible course. One of the sessions in this course is an exercise in reading the Bible from the margins. After a brief introduction, participants are given three passages from the gospels with their traditional interpretations, together with a few questions that cast doubt on these and invite fresh engagement with the texts. This generally provokes very lively group discussion before findings are shared. Some participants are unconvinced by fresh interpretations; others have found these persuasive and liberating. One participant declared: 'I am furious!' I assumed he was offended by my daring to question established interpretations, but actually he was outraged that nobody had offered him alternative perspectives like this before.

Transitioning to minority status, we can embrace the opportunity to do theology in fresh ways and read the Bible from a different perspective. As we remove the blinkers we have worn for many centuries in a dominant, if nominal, Christian culture, all kinds of discoveries await us. Reading the Bible from the margins does not mean discounting or devaluing the interpretive work of generations of gifted biblical scholars. But it does mean embracing a 'hermeneutics of suspicion' regarding the influence upon them of majority Christian status and welcoming the opportunity to delve afresh into the Scriptures as we ask what it means to be followers of Jesus in a changing culture.

Gospel and culture

Are we in danger, though, of being unduly influenced by the surrounding culture in which we are now a minority? Yes, of course. And there are parts of the Christian community that seem to have fallen into this trap and are losing their identity. But the opposite danger is to cling on fearfully or doggedly to past formulations and practices without subjecting them to adequate scrutiny. Are they truly biblical or are they the result of undue influence from the culture that is now fading? If we are to avoid stumbling too far in either direction, we will need to resist the temptation to label others dismissively as 'liberal' or 'conservative' (or harsher epithets) and listen carefully to different viewpoints.

And in a minority community we will need to think like cross-cultural missionaries. As those who live in other cultures than their own know, the relationship between gospel and culture is always under negotiation. Cultures are not static and many of them are complex. The gospel needs to be incarnated and expressed in various ways if it is to be perceived and received as good news in different contexts. Gospel values and priorities affirm some aspects of culture and challenge others. The Christian community is to be culturally attuned but also counter-cultural in its lifestyle and the message it conveys. And in a complex, rapidly evolving and kaleidoscopic culture with multiple subcultures, contextualization is a never-ending task. But this kind of flexibility and provisionality was alien to a majority Christian community, which assumed that the relationship between gospel and culture had long ago been settled and that there was no need to revisit this.

As in the previous section, there is space only for examples of what this might mean.[26] But as we think about the relationship between the gospel and our culture, one of the basic issues we must confront is what actually represents 'good news' in our society. The biblical narrative is incredibly rich and offers us extraordinary resources, so it is disappointing when the gospel is reduced to simplistic formulae or circumscribed by requirements that it is presented in certain well-worn ways. The classic approach in Western societies is to concentrate on human sin and guilt and present good news of justification through the work of Christ, forgiveness of sin and a clear conscience before God. Christendom has been described as a 'guilt culture' and in this context justification, forgiveness and freedom from guilt are wonderfully good

---

[26] But the Gospel and Our Culture Network has been working on this for many years and their website has extensive resources on this subject. See http://www.gospel-culture.org.uk.

news. But not all societies are 'guilt cultures'. Other presenting issues are more significant in these contexts.

Some societies, especially in the Middle East and much of Asia, might better be described as 'shame cultures'. Others, in parts of Africa and elsewhere, might qualify as 'fear cultures'. In these contexts, guilt is less troubling than it has been to many Western consciences, but shame or fear can be crippling. What, then, is the good news in these cultures? How does the gospel address the issues of shame and fear? Those who ask this question and search the Bible for resources find, often to their surprise, that these are major biblical themes and that there are numerous stories and texts that address these concerns.[27] The popular saying applies that 'for a man with a hammer everything looks like a nail'.[28] If our only lens is sin–guilt–justification–forgiveness, we tend to find only what we are looking for. But the gospel is bigger, richer and more liberating than this. It is good news in all cultures and addresses all aspects of our fallen human condition.

Embracing a more holistic gospel is crucial for a minority Christian community in Western societies for two reasons. First, we now have many more friends, neighbours and colleagues from 'shame' and 'fear' cultures. Second, post-Christendom is not a 'guilt culture' in the way that Christendom was. Research confirms what we already know. John Finney reported over twenty years ago, when he was the archbishop's officer for the Decade of Evangelism, that 'four-fifths of people coming to faith did not find the cross and forgiveness the most appealing part of faith'.[29] And more

---

[27] For instance, on shame, see Gen. 2:25; Pss 25:2,3,20; 31:1,17; 69:6,7,19; Isa. 45:17; 54:4; 61:7; Rom. 9:33; 10:11; Heb. 12:2; Rev. 21:27. On fear, see Pss 3:5–7; 23:4; 27:1–4; 91:4–6; Isa. 35:4; 41:10–14; John 20:19; Rom. 8:15; Heb. 2:15. On shame and fear combined, see 1 Sam. 15:30; Job 10:15; 31:11; Ps. 91:15; Isa. 54:14; Zeph. 3:15–16; 1 John 4:18. Examples of salvation from shame include Gomer (in Hosea), Zacchaeus, Mary Magdalene and Peter. Examples of salvation from fear include Joshua, Nehemiah and the disciples in the upper room.

[28] This saying, sometimes known as 'Maslow's hammer', is attributed to psychologist Abraham Maslow, but has several variants that predate his book, *The Psychology of Science* (New York: Harper Row, 1966).

[29] John Finney, *Emerging Evangelism* (London: Darton, Longman & Todd, 2004), p. 90.

recently interviewers asking what the 'big questions' were that people wanted to talk about discovered no interest at all in guilt.[30] The traditional gospel message simply does not sound like good news to many people in our society.

Two caveats are important at this point. First, when anthropologists designate a society as a 'guilt culture', 'shame culture' or 'fear culture', they are not suggesting that these are the only concerns in that society. In all human cultures guilt, shame and fear are concerns. But in most societies one or other of these is the dominant and presenting concern. Second, it does not follow from these observations that those who do not feel guilty are not guilty. Sin and guilt are realities for all human beings.

Challenging the traditional sin–guilt–justification–forgiveness paradigm can be problematic as it risks accusations of watering down the gospel. But if we are to be effective cross-cultural missionaries in a complex and changing culture we dare not be cowed by such accusations or in thrall to reductionist approaches. A gospel that addresses the issues of shame and fear is no less biblical, no less Christ-centred and no less cruciform than that which addresses the issue of guilt. Genesis 3 reveals that the primal act of disobedience resulted in a human condition characterized by shame and fear as well as guilt: 'I was afraid, because I was naked; and I hid myself', says Adam (v. 10). And these three issues come together in a classic New Testament text on the work of Christ on the cross:

> And when you were dead in trespasses and the uncircumcision of your flesh, God made you alive together with him, when he forgave us all our trespasses, erasing the record that stood against us with its legal demands. He set this aside, nailing it to the cross. He disarmed the rulers and authorities and made a public example of them, triumphing over them in it. (Col. 2:13–15)

God has in Christ forgiven our sins, removed our guilt, triumphed over the enemies we feared and transferred our shame to them. The gospel addresses all these issues. We are not at liberty to omit any of them, but we are free to prioritize those which connect most powerfully in our context. This is what missiologists call 'contextualization'

---

[30] Steven Croft et al., *Evangelism in a Spiritual Age* (London: Church House Publishing, 2005), p. 17.

– a standard practice in most other societies but still in its infancy in Western societies.

Eddie Gibbs, professor of church growth at Fuller Theological Seminary, argues that our task is no different from that of the early disciples. He writes:

> In missiological language, Paul's approach represents contextualization, which requires great discernment, under the guidance of the Holy Spirit and in ongoing conversation with the people concerned. The gospel message is not compromised in order to remove the offence of the unique claims of Christ and the significance of the cross and his resurrection; rather, the message is interpreted in order to relate to the distinctive issues in a particular culture.[31]

There are rich resources in the global Christian community from which we can learn as we explore these issues. Some Western missiologists are also offering fresh perspectives.[32] But we have much further to go. What is good news for the abused, addicted and sinned against? What about the happy, moral secularist or the crusading social activist? How does the gospel address despair, loneliness, alienation and meaninglessness? And how does it intersect with aspirations rather than needs? A majority Christian community might represent itself as a dispenser of answers to needs, but needs-based evangelism may be less appropriate for a minority community. What if we invited others to join a revolutionary movement, a band of pilgrims, a community with quite different values and priorities than the rest of society? Of course, this would mean at least aspiring to be such a community . . .

And all of the above is concerned with the needs and aspirations of human beings, whereas the life, death and resurrection of Christ have cosmic dimensions and point forward to 'the renewal

[31] Eddie Gibbs, *The Rebirth of the Church* (Grand Rapids: Baker, 2013), p. 104.

[32] Some are proposing changes of terminology without really addressing more fundamental issues. An example is Laurence Singlehurst, *The Gospel Message Today: Language that Connects in Communicating the Gospel* (Cambridge: Grove Books, 2013). Others are wrestling with the theological categories, such as Alan Mann, *Atonement for a 'Sinless' Society: Engaging with an Emerging Culture* (Carlisle: Authentic, 2005).

of all things' to which Jesus looked forward[33] and 'the time of universal restoration that God announced long ago through his holy prophets'.[34] The gospel is much more glorious and multidimensional than standard presentations suggest, and our understanding of the mission of God can no longer be restricted to saving souls, enlarging congregations or presiding over a supposedly Christianized society. The vocation of a minority Christian community is not only to be creative but to be prophetic.

---

[33] Matt. 19:28.
[34] Acts 3:21.

6.

A Prophetic Ministry

Missio Dei

An early indication that the Christian community in Western societies was beginning to grapple with the implications of minority status was the recovery in the middle years of the twentieth century of the concept of *missio Dei*. Karl Barth, at a missionary conference in Brandenburg in 1932, insisted that *missio* was 'an expression of the doctrine of the Trinity – namely an expression of the divine sending forth of the self, the sending of the Son and the Holy Spirit to the world'. This was the understanding of mission in the early church. *Missio* was used to describe the way in which the Father sent the Son and the Spirit into the world. The church is caught up in this mission flow: 'as the Father has sent me, so I send you' (John 20:21). But the church is not the 'sender' but the 'sent'. God is the sender. Then, in 1952 at another missionary conference in Willingen, Karl Hartenstein picked up Barth's contention and introduced the term *missio Dei* – God's mission. This deceptively simple term, which reminds us that mission flows from the heart of God and embraces all that God purposes for creation, has explosive consequences.

For many centuries the Christian community in Europe operated with a defective and highly distorted understanding of mission:

- It meant going beyond the boundaries of Christendom to convert people and bring them within the orbit of a dominant church.
- It was left to specialists and was not perceived as something most Christians had any responsibility towards, except through providing financial support.

- It usually involved cultural imposition because the missionaries were rarely able or willing to differentiate between the gospel and its embodiment in European culture.
- It might employ some measure of coercion, sometimes violence, which was justified on the grounds that 'error has no rights'.
- It had little relevance within the boundaries of Christendom, now officially regarded as evangelized, so the pioneering ministries of apostles, prophets and evangelists were redundant.
- It was a responsibility of the church authorities, a church programme which God was invited to endorse and bless.
- Its goals were to save souls from damnation and to expand the reach and influence of God's kingdom, which was equated with the institutional church.

Minority Christian communities periodically questioned or rejected this approach. Some were unconvinced that Christendom was authentically Christian and engaged in evangelism within its boundaries. Some recovered the ministries of apostles, prophets and evangelists, and urged all their members to take responsibility for mission. Some rejected any form of coercion and pioneered the idea of religious liberty. And some missionaries sent beyond the boundaries of Christendom discovered that the gospel could be embodied in new ways within other cultures and need not be encumbered by all the trappings of European culture.

These historic minority perspectives, which once provoked persecution, are now very widely accepted, even if we are still working through the implications. The recovery of *missio Dei*, initially in academic circles but increasingly at a more popular level, and the ubiquity of the term 'missional', have underscored this. We are now persuaded, at least in principle, that mission is not a church programme but a divine initiative, energized and directed by the Holy Spirit, in which the Christian community is invited to join. We acknowledge that mission is the calling, privilege and responsibility of *all* followers of Jesus. It is not restricted to certain organized activities of the 'gathered' church, but involves witness as a 'dispersed' community throughout the week and in all aspects of our lives. We are starting to recognize and train women and men with pioneering ministries, recovering the neglected roles of apostles and prophets, even if we are not yet sure how to define or deploy these. We realize that in a plural society mission must be respectful of the views of others and in all contexts must be ethical, utterly averse to manipulation. And we are aware that mission is now 'from everywhere to everywhere' and that 'reverse mission' is becoming a significant feature in Western societies, as missionaries from Africa, Asia and Latin America respond to a sense of indebtedness and embrace the challenge of re-evangelizing nations from which missionaries were once sent to their forebears.[1]

These are important gains. They represent an expression of humility more appropriate for a minority community than the arrogant missiology of previous generations. They amount to a reorientation and recalibration of the Christian community that will better equip us to engage creatively and, as we will argue, prophetically with a culture that is deeply suspicious of any kind of 'mission' and intolerant of evangelistic programmes, products and antics. Two other theological terms that have become increasingly popular in recent years may, if interpreted in conjunction with *missio Dei*, offer additional way markers on the missional journey. These are 'incarnation' and 'the kingdom of God'.

But familiarity with theological concepts and the adoption of 'missional' terminology will not guarantee the transformation required for a minority Christian community. Paradigm shifts of this kind require sustained attention, persistent reinforcement, different institutional priorities and ways of measuring progress, and practical implementation at a local level. George Lings warns: 'Pastoral mode is like a dominant gene. It is reproduced in the next generation with little effort. However, being missional is like a recessive gene and the perennial danger is that it will be bred out in the next generation.' The Christian community has operated in pastoral mode for centuries, so he concludes, 'To eclipse mission, all that is needed is to do nothing.'[2]

Michael Frost, a leading 'missional church' advocate, has expressed deep concern that this language is being misused and

---

[1] See further the developing work of the Centre for Missionaries from the Majority World: http://www.cmmw.org.

[2] George Lings, *Encounters on the Edge 41* (Sheffield: Sheffield Centre, 2009), pp. 10–11.

that often there is only superficial change. He contends that too many 'remain resolutely committed to the existing paradigm while recommending we add a certain missional, shall we say, *flavor* to the mix . . . that we can flavor all our existing programs to be missional without having to renegotiate anything central or core to the current paradigm'.[3] He is also concerned that 'missional' does not become simply another word for 'evangelistic'. At risk of going over familiar ground, then, maybe we need to explore further the implications of *missio Dei* and the connotations of incarnation and the kingdom of God.

Picking up the discussion at the end of the previous chapter about the scope of the gospel, our commitment to and outworking of these theological themes precludes narrow, individualized, disembodied or institutional strategies and expectations. For *missio Dei* is the great plan of God, the dream of God for the creation God loved into being. It involves 'the restoration of all things' (Acts 3:21), the establishing of the prophetic hope of *shalom*. It invites us to savour the prospect of a redeemed humanity within a renewed cosmos. Participating in God's mission, then, as indicated in an earlier chapter, can lead us to become involved in a wide range of activities: evangelism, working for justice, care for creation, political activism, church planting, education, reconciling enemies, cultural renewal, healing minds and bodies, offering hope and imagination.

But we need more than a checklist of activities. We need what Walter Brueggemann calls 'prophetic imagination'[4] if we are to sustain hope and have a compelling vision to commend to a jaded culture. We need to see what prophets like Isaiah saw as they dreamed of a world made whole. Five times the prophet imagines the holy mountain of God as the scene of ultimate reconciliation and restoration. This is what *shalom* looks like.

In the first scene (Isa. 2:1–4), he sees many nations going up together to this mountain, to learn God's ways, nations no longer in dispute and not needing weapons of war any longer and so transforming them into agricultural tools. This passage is one of the most frequently quoted biblical texts in early

---

[3] Michael Frost, *The Road to Missional* (Grand Rapids: Baker, 2011), p. 17.

[4] See, among other places, Walter Brueggemann, *The Prophetic Imagination* (Minneapolis: Fortress Press, 2001).

Christian writings, expressing the hope and longing of that minority community.

In the second scene (Isa. 11:6–9), the prophet's vision of reconciliation has expanded to embrace the animal kingdom as well as humanity as he imagines wolves and lambs taking a nap together and a child playing unharmed with snakes. He declares that there will be no hurt or destruction on the holy mountain and anticipates the earth being as full of the knowledge of the Lord as the waters cover the sea.

In the third scene (Isa. 25:6–9), the prophet imagines a glorious picnic being spread out on the mountain to which all the nations are invited – one of many biblical passages that speak of a great feast or banquet to usher in the new age. There will be no more disgrace or sorrow, he assures us, as tears are wiped away and death itself is swallowed up for ever.

In the fourth scene (Isa. 56:6–8), he returns to the theme of reconciliation between nations and declares that the holy mountain is to be home for non-Israelites who join themselves to the Lord. This is a scene of homecoming for refugees as scattered Israelites and members of other nations wend their way to the mountain and bring their worship to the God who gathers and welcomes them. This mountain, the prophet insists and Jesus later reminds us, will be 'a house of prayer for all nations'.

The fifth scene (Isa. 65:17–25), much longer than the others, recapitulates many of these themes and images, promising that the holy mountain will be the site of God's blessing and God's presence, a place of security, community and joy. Isaiah speaks of God's intention to 'create new heavens and a new earth'. *Missio Dei* not only guides our missiology and shapes our ecclesiology; it determines our eschatology. Our gospel is not escapist, either in the sense of extracting us from our social networks and contemporary responsibilities or in promoting the utterly inadequate ambition of going to heaven rather than inhabiting the 'new heavens and a new earth'. And our mandate is to be a prophetic minority, keeping alive the rumour of this extraordinary hope and dropping hints to encourage others to imagine a different world.

Brueggemann suggests that to sustain such 'prophetic imagination' the Christian community needs to value the ministry of poets, who can offer fresh perspectives and counter the dulling influence of what he calls a 'prose-flattened world'.[5] A powerful example of this that I have shared with many groups is Doug Gay's poem, 'A New Glasgow', in which he imagines the trans-formational impact on his city of the New Jerusalem descending there. Taking familiar images from Revelation 21 – 22, the poet invites his readers to see Glasgow in a new light: 'I saw Glasgow, the holy city, coming down out of heaven, shining like a rare jewel, sparkling like clear water in the eye of the sun, and all the sickness was gone from the city, and there were no more suburbs and schemes, no difference between Bearsden and Drumchapel.'[6] This poem, which explores what *shalom* would look like locally, has not only frequently reduced listeners to tears but has also inspired similar prophetic poems imagining what East London, Leeds, Bradford, Belfast, Southend and other cities might be like when the kingdom of God has fully come.

Incarnation and the Kingdom of God

The visions of Isaiah are awesome and winsome, but the term 'kingdom' is problematic in contemporary culture, redolent of hierarchy, domination, institution and demarcated territory. This is something to which a minority Christian community needs to be attuned. Some have coined 'kindom' as a relational alternative; others have proposed 'the unkingdom of God' to signal its very different values.[7] If we continue to use the traditional term, which is so central to the teaching of Jesus in the gospels, we must acknowl-edge these difficulties and take care to differentiate God's reign

---

5 Walter Brueggemann, in *The Prophetic Imagination* and also in *Finally Comes the Poet* (Minneapolis: Augsburg Fortress, 1989). Other books which commend the role of the poet include Eddie Gibbs, *Church Next* (Downers Grove: IVP, 2001); and Alan Roxburgh, *The Missionary Congregation, Leadership, and Liminality* (New York: Continuum, 1997).

6 The poem can be found in Jonny Baker and Doug Gay, *Alternative Worship* (London: SPCK, 2003), pp. 94–5.

7 See, for example, *The Inclusive New Testament* (Lanham: AltaMira Press, 2004); and Mark Van Steenwyk, *The Unkingdom of God: Embracing the Subversive Power of Repentance* (Downers Grove: IVP, 2013).

from that of other authorities. We might introduce the idea of an 'upside-down kingdom'[8] or speak more often about *shalom*, the Old Testament equivalent to the kingdom of God in the New Testament.

How is our understanding of *missio Dei* enriched by the concept of the kingdom of God, and how does this equip us as a prophetic minority? A declining ex-majority community can be unhealthily fixated on its own organizations, resources and congregations – on their survival or capacity to influence society. But the kingdom of God is not to be equated with the church. The church is a sign of the kingdom – a foretaste, a sacrament, a provisional representation, a pale foreshadowing of the eschatological reality to which it witnesses. The church is an agent of the kingdom – an instrument of the kingdom, in possession of the 'keys' of the kingdom, as it imperfectly but persistently proclaims and demonstrates the coming of the kingdom. But God's kingdom is not limited to the vision, resources and activities of the church.

This has several practical implications:

- It alerts us to the humbling reality that the church is not always at the forefront of the mission of God, but may be well off the pace. God's kingdom advances sometimes in spite of the church, beyond the church and towards the church.
- It delivers pioneers from the ridiculous assumption that they bring God with them into communities, neighbourhoods or networks. It liberates them to discover what God has been doing there before they arrived and to get involved in this.
- It warns us to expect the unexpected, especially if we read the Bible with eyes open to the many occasions when God's purposes advanced through outsiders, those on the margins and other unlikely people, such as Jethro, Rahab, Cyrus, Mary, Cornelius and others.
- It invites us to explore fruitful partnerships with agencies, communities, organizations and individuals who may not acknowledge Jesus as Lord but exhibit 'kingdom values' in their relationships, activities and concern for social transformation.
- If we embrace the idea of an upside-down kingdom, this encourages us to forsake the perspective that we need large

---

8   As in the excellent book by Donald Kraybill, *The Upside-Down Kingdom* (Scottdale: Herald Press, 2011).

churches to exercise public influence, well-connected church leaders to gain the attention of policy-makers, or glossy advertising campaigns to attract people to church programmes and events. We might instead prioritize grass-roots initiatives and ministry on the margins of society.

The term 'incarnation' is problematic for other reasons than those associated with 'kingdom' language, especially when used in its adjectival form. 'Incarnational', appended to ministry, mission or lifestyle, has become very popular but has been interpreted in so many ways that it is in danger of becoming debased:

- Living locally, rather than engaging in mission from a safe distance;
- Participating in the community, rather than remaining aloof from it;
- Affirming and valuing all we can in the local culture;
- Being self-aware and sensitive to our own assumptions and prejudices;
- Believing that God is already at work in the community and joining in;
- Concentrating on relationships rather than programmes;
- Interpreting mission as 'go to them' rather than 'come to us' (attractional);
- Operating from the grass roots rather than from positions of power;
- Embodying the gospel through small groups that infuse society;
- Doing things with rather than for the community;
- Communicating the gospel in contextual language and images;
- Communicating the gospel through deeds as well as words;
- Understanding faith and discipleship as whole-life activities;
- Rejecting sacred/secular dualism and refusing to see church as a separate sphere;
- Not knowing in advance what our ministry will lead to;
- Regarding mission as two-way, so that we learn as much as we teach;
- Not extracting new believers from their culture but equipping them to live within it as followers of Jesus;

- Operating as 'salt' and 'leaven' in the community;
- Working for cultural transformation from the inside rather than the outside.

Many of these definitions of 'incarnational mission' are important for a minority community and aspects of its prophetic role within society, but we should highlight some concerns. One of these is the validity of using incarnational language without threatening the uniqueness of Jesus Christ as the incarnate Son of God and developing some kind of messiah-complex. Can we really justify using incarnational language to explain our decision to shop locally rather than at the superstore in order to identify with the local community, when the same language is used to describe Jesus not claiming equality with God but emptying himself and taking the form of a servant in order to redeem humanity? There are, however, biblical encouragements to extend the language of incarnation in this direction. When Jesus told his disciples 'as the Father has sent me, so I am sending you', this implies that the disciples are to embody his continuing mission and ministry. Paul refers to the church as the 'body of Christ' on many occasions – his favourite image for the church – and the New Testament uses language that indicates the ascended Christ is the head of this body, directing and energizing its activities.'[9]

Michael Frost acknowledges the concern that the uniqueness of the incarnation of Jesus is not compromised and explains: 'I am not suggesting we are all Christs, far from it! I am asking us to be open to being filled by the Spirit of the incarnate One, to pattern our lives on his example and to commit ourselves to participate in God's work of bringing history to its true end.'[10] Perhaps, then, we can extend the language of incarnation – with care – to the mission of God's people.

But if we do so, we must ensure this language does not become generic and disconnected from the biblical narrative. The focal point of *missio Dei* is the life, death and resurrection of Jesus. The incarnation was the sending of the Son by the Father in the power

---

[9] Eph. 4:7–16 and elsewhere.
[10] Michael Frost, *Incarnate: The Body of Christ in an Age of Disengagement* (Downers Grove: IVP, 2014), p. 87. See further, Darrell Guder, *The Incarnation and the Church's Witness* (Eugene, OR: Wipf & Stock, 1999).

of the Spirit to announce the kingdom of God and bring it near. Although it is the term *missio Dei* that has become popular, we might equally speak about *missio Trinitatis*. As Jürgen Moltmann writes, 'It is not the church that has a mission of salvation to fulfil in the world; it is the mission of the Son and the Spirit through the Father that includes the church.'[11] This means that the anointing of the Spirit that empowered Jesus' ministry must also empower ours. And the means by which Jesus pursued his mission are the means by which we are to participate in God's mission. This implies renouncing all missional activities that are incompatible with the way of Jesus and embracing the way of the cross. And it means learning from the life of Jesus as well as proclaiming his death and resurrection.

Incarnation points in two directions. Jesus was incarnate as he fully identified with humanity, living as a first-century Jew who spoke Aramaic and probably some Greek; attended the local synagogue; went to weddings and parties; laughed and wept with his friends; was angered by injustice; and suffered at the hands of the political and religious authorities. But Jesus was also incarnate because he embodied God, taught and lived out the ways of God's kingdom, challenged those around him to embrace the values of God's kingdom, and ministered God's liberation and healing. Incarnational mission, if Jesus is our example, means identifying with and being fully present within our neighbourhoods and networks but also representing God, telling the 'big story' of God's purposes, and challenging dimensions of our culture that are not consistent with these purposes. Incarnational mission involves speaking as well as being, critique as well as affirmation, prophecy as well as pastoral sensitivity.

The vocation of the Christian community, then, as a minority in a society fast losing its grip on the story that definitively (though not exclusively) shaped Western culture and seemingly bereft of any hopeful alternative story, is to live out and speak out the story of *missio Dei*. If we are to do this with integrity, humility and confidence, what we do when we meet together must shape and equip us for this task. We need to rehearse the 'big story'. We need to sing songs that inspire prophetic imagination. We need to share

[11] Jürgen Moltmann, *The Church in the Power of the Spirit* (London: SCM, 2000), p. 64.

and hear testimonies that report signs of God's kingdom in daily life. We need to develop a missional hermeneutics as we read the Bible together. We need to help each other discern which aspect of God's mission we are called to be involved in. We need to affirm the missional dimension of all areas of our daily lives and provide opportunities to reflect together on these. And we need to do these things in such a way that we do not exhaust each other with our gatherings but release each other to be fully engaged in incarnational mission and ministry. No wonder the advocates of 'missional church' are not convinced we have yet reached this goal!

Peace

What are the priorities, then, for a prophetic minority? In what ways might we point towards the new world we have glimpsed and offer fresh perspectives and a compelling vision?

Two of the most fundamental human concerns in a fallen world are provision and protection. We no longer enjoy the abundance and security of Eden. We are anxious about our resources and our possessions, and we are fearful of enemies who threaten us and everything we have. In Chapter 4 we explored economic aspects of discipleship, noting the way economic issues dominate the news media and thereby our cultural imagination, and suggested that progress in this area might have a knock-on effect in other areas. Here, we suggest that reflecting on how we respond to those we consider our enemies might be equally fruitful.

This chapter was taking shape in the week an American journalist was beheaded by Islamist militiamen who regard Western nations as their enemies. Although many other journalists and numerous civilians have been treated just as brutally, this incident received global attention, not least because a Western journalist was the victim and the executioner was apparently from Britain. Western governments declared the militant group responsible to be the biggest threat they had faced for many years and warned that the streets of Western cities might be the sites of such atrocities in the near future. In the same week, the fragile truce in Gaza evaporated and the seemingly interminable conflict between Israelis and Palestinians resumed. Fighting continued in Syria, where an estimated 191,000 people have died, and in Iraq and Afghanistan. The conflict in Eastern Ukraine was unresolved as the bodies of passengers killed by a missile aimed at a passenger plane flying over the country were returned to Malaysia. And these were just the war zones that made the headlines in that week. Many others were no longer 'news' – and these will not be 'news' by the time this paragraph is read. And they are, of course, only the latest outbreaks of hatred, violence and retaliation that have plagued human society for millennia.

Responses to these dreadful incidents, ongoing conflicts and perceived threats are predictable and understandable. Governments promise protection through increased surveillance, border controls, military action and unspecified measures. US President Obama vowed: 'We will do everything we can to protect our people and the timeless values that we stand for.'[12] Adding a comment no British politician would likely make, he declared: 'No just God would stand for what they did yesterday and what they do every single day.' This theological statement is not only a reminder that our 'vast minority' analysis cannot be transposed without qualifications into the American context. It also invites reflection on how God might view these situations and what a just God might want done about them.

My intention here is not to pass judgement on the policies and actions of governments, but to reflect on the role of a minority Christian community in a violent world. The early Christians were in no doubt that Jesus' teaching about loving their enemies precluded their participation in war, endorsement of judicial executions, approval of aborting babies, and any other forms of violence. They were often accused of enjoying the protection of the empire and its armies without shouldering any responsibility for its defence, but they insisted that theirs was a different vocation. Inspired by the biblical vision of weapons of war being transformed into agricultural implements, they devoted themselves to living towards this vision and forming communities that, albeit imperfectly, anticipated the peaceful kingdom to which the

---

[12] Reported at http://www.nbcnews.com/storyline/james-foley/obama-journalists-killing-no-just-god-would-stand-what-they-n185076.

prophets looked forward.[13] This was how the original minority Christian community interpreted Jesus' teaching and perceived their role.

As this community grew and eventually became a majority in an empire threatened from all sides, it became more sensitive to the accusation that it was irresponsible in a violent world to refuse to fight. Dealing with criminality and insurrection also seemed to require firm action and punitive measures. And the Christian community now exercised much greater influence and had much more invested in the status quo. Perhaps their vocation had changed. Vestiges of the older approach remained and memories of this inspired dissident groups, unconvinced by the new mainstream orthodoxy. But the Christian community learned to interpret biblical teaching in ways that no longer outlawed the use of violence in just causes and allowed it to play a full part in the society it now dominated. Although debate persists over the legitimacy of this revisionist interpretation, few doubt that the changing status and role of the Christian community significantly impacted the way it read the Bible and the ethical stance it adopted.

As a minority Christian community today considers its vocation in a violent world, we have a responsibility to assess the mixed legacy of past centuries. Do we exercise whatever influence we still have to defend the continuing use of violent means in the cause of justice (however this is defined), but perhaps to encourage moderation and restraint? Or do we renounce our support for and complicity in violence, not only because religion in general and Christianity in particular is castigated for this, but because we no longer believe this is compatible with the teachings of Jesus? How do we interpret the wealth of material, not all of which seems to point in the same direction, when we read the Bible from the margins? Should we adopt as more appropriate for a minority community the perspective of the early Christians and many dissident groups? If so, does this consign us to irrelevance and open us afresh to accusations of irresponsibility, or can we offer something distinctive and creative? Within the Christian

---

[13] One of the most widely quoted biblical texts in the early centuries was Isa. 2:4. See further, Alan Kreider, Eleanor Kreider and Paulus Widjaja, *A Culture of Peace: God's Vision for the Church* (Intercourse, PA: Good Books, 2005).

community there are not only divergent views but frequently a reluctance to address what is perceived as a divisive issue. Even if the commemorations of the First World War scheduled during the next few years provoke greater discussion,[14] there is no realistic prospect of the Christian community speaking with a united voice any time soon. And whatever we decide, most of our contemporaries will take some persuading that we might have anything worthwhile to contribute.

Rather than pontificating, then, a minority Christian community might invest its energies in exploring and supporting creative peaceful alternatives to institutions, policies and practices that do not seem to be working well, such as:

- Restorative justice initiatives that bring victims and offenders together and focus on reconciliation and restitution rather than retribution. Several programmes are running in Britain alongside traditional elements of the criminal justice system and evidence is mounting of their positive outcomes, in the face of considerable scepticism and some opposition.[15] Christians have been deeply involved in the development of restorative justice principles and practices,[16] and the Christian community has the capacity as 'a vast minority' to support these initiatives, advocate for their extension, and pioneer other alternatives to current criminal justice policies that are dehumanizing, expensive and ineffective. Creative alternatives to imprisonment are desperately needed.
- Christian peacemaker teams that are deployed in conflict situations at the invitation of local peacemaking communities.

[14] An example in November 2014 was a debate in London on the subject 'Who would Jesus shoot?' between Nigel Biggar, author of *In Defence of War* (Oxford: Oxford University Press, 2013) and Tom Yoder Neufeld, author of *Jesus and the Subversion of Violence* (London: SPCK, 2011).

[15] See http://www.restorativesolutions.org.uk. As this chapter was being written, there was news of substantial funding for restorative justice initiatives based on encouraging research findings.

[16] For example, Howard Zehr, *Changing Lenses: A New Focus for Crime and Justice* (Scottdale: Herald Press, 2005) and *The Little Book of Restorative Justice* (Intercourse, PA: Good Books, 2002); and Christopher Marshall, *Compassionate Justice* (Eugene, OR: Wipf & Stock, 2012).

These teams are committed to supporting grass-roots initiatives, 'building partnerships to transform violence and oppression', 'embodying creative non-violence and liberating love,' and 'waging nonviolent direct action to confront systems of violence and oppression.'[17] These teams are representatives of a growing movement of Third Party Nonviolent Intervention organizations, only some of which are Christian in ethos, which are challenging the widely held assumption that violent intervention or doing nothing are the only alternatives in the face of injustice and oppression. Another example is the Christian International Peace Service.[18]

- Supporting the 'just peacemaking' initiative, developed under the leadership of Glen Stassen and based at Fuller Theological Seminary. This is an attempt to move beyond debates between pacifists and those who support 'just war' by focusing on practical ways of preventing wars. It promotes ten practices of peacemaking, gathers examples of their implementation and encourages further research.[19]

- Drawing attention to initiatives such as the Conflict Pool, a programme involving three UK government departments that funds conflict prevention, stabilization and peace-keeping activities, and urging much greater investment in this and reporting of outcomes.[20]

- Advocating for an equivalent to Armed Forces Day for those involved in peaceful conflict resolution, and encouraging denominations that have military chaplains to provide chaplains to 'peace forces' and non-violent initiatives.[21]

- Joining Conscience in its campaign for 'a progressive increase in the amount of UK tax spent on peace-building, and a corresponding decrease in the amount spent on war and preparation for war'. Conscience also campaigns for 'the legal right of those with a conscientious objection to war

---

[17] See http://www.cpt.org.

[18] See http://www.chipspeace.org.

[19] See further Glen Stassen, *Just Peacemaking: The New Paradigm for the Ethics of Peace and War* (Cleveland, OH: Pilgrim Press, 2009) and http://justpeacemaking.org.

[20] See http://www.gov.uk/government/publications/conflict-pool.

[21] See http://http://www.ekklesia.co.uk/node/20056.

to have the entire military part of their taxes spent on peace-building'.[22]

- Disseminating and encouraging reflection on the 'modest proposal for peace' made by John Stoner in 1984: 'Let the Christians of the world agree that they will not kill each other.' This seemingly innocuous proposal has all kinds of ramifications and provides a creative starting point for conversations around issues of nationalism, violence and the global Christian community.

The Christian community might also model good listening and peaceful conversations around contentious issues as an alternative to the oppositional and adversarial culture that dominates politics and the media. A cursory scan of comments on news websites and blogs indicates that antagonism, caricature, abuse, hostility and unwillingness to respond graciously to other views is endemic and makes these exchanges dysfunctional and depressing. If the Christian community can develop and model the ethos and attributes of attentive listening, creative conversation (rather than debate or even discussion) and genuine respect for conversation partners with whom there is passionate disagreement, this might be a powerful witness to the reconciling power of the gospel.

Division and discord within many sections of the Christian community, and frequent requests for help from organizations like Bridge Builders,[23] suggest we have some way to go before we have much to offer others. But building a culture of peace within the Christian community is vital for our own future and might be a gift to a conflicted society. Bridge Builders believe that 'the church is called to be an authentic sign of the kingdom of God by expressing the reconciling, community-creating love of God' and 'practical peace-making and blessing of one's enemies are core elements of the Christian gospel'. They want to see 'people looking on curiously at the church and saying, "so that's what reconciliation looks like in practice."'

These are just a handful of examples of active and creative peace-making – a far cry from the uninvolved pacifism that is so often castigated as the 'do nothing' alternative to violent and punitive

[22] See http://www.conscienceonline.org.uk.
[23] See http://www.bbministries.org.uk.

action. They take with utmost seriousness the conflicted and violent realities of the world. They are inspired, motivated and sustained by the reconciliation that is at the heart of the gospel and by the prophetic vision of peace throughout the entire creation (the hope of *shalom*). This means we need not be hamstrung by desperation to be successful or effective in the short term – which releases creativity and allows for risk-taking. And if a 'vast minority' lives like this and bears credible witness to this compelling vision, it might be good news in a society desperately short of genuine hope.

What if?

In the same week in which this chapter was being written and news of the brutal execution in Iraq was making headlines, I was encouraged to read a short article by Steve Clifford, general director of the Evangelical Alliance, which claims to represent two million Christians in the UK. Reflecting on conflict situations around the world, he wondered whether there might be a better way of responding than the West's aggressive militarism. He recounted the story of the Amish of Nickel Mines (which we told in Chapter 4) and quoted twice from the Sermon on the Mount as Jesus pronounced blessing on the peacemakers and instructed his disciples to turn the other cheek. And he asked 'what if' the response to the attack on 11 September 2001 had been inspired by Jesus' teaching and, instead of repaying evil with evil, had been to reach out to moderate Muslims and invest, not in weapons of war, but in health care, education and other forms of support for poor communities who are often susceptible to extremism. Might such a surprising response have resulted in fewer deaths, fewer recruits for terrorism, reduced tension and a safer world?[24]

Although others have made similar suggestions since 2001, Steve Clifford's article was encouraging for two reasons. First, the evangelical constituency, a growing sector of the Christian community in Britain, has often been preoccupied with issues of sexual morality and has not been known for its advocacy of non-violence and enemy-loving. Might this brief article stimulate further reflection in this community on the implications of Jesus'

[24] *IDEA* (September/October 2014), p. 38.

teaching on these subjects? Second, the tone of the article is appropriate for a spokesperson from a minority community. Asking 'what if?' offers an alternative perspective, invites dialogue, and engages the imagination. This is much more winsome than pontificating, moralizing and sermonizing. If the Christian community adopts this approach and speaks in this tone, others will be more inclined to listen and engage with us.

'What if?' is a question a prophetic minority poses. The Christian community can no longer assert its views from the perspective of a moral majority, peppering these with 'oughts' and 'shoulds'. We do not have the social standing, spiritual authority or credibility to claim this status. Nor will such pronouncements be received with enthusiasm or make any significant impact on policy-makers or public opinion. Furthermore, most pronouncements of this kind tend to be dull, worthy and predictable, rather than creative, provocative and imaginative. If we want to contribute effectively to public debates, we need to do so as a prophetic minority, asking unexpected questions and offering intriguing alternatives.

This change of tone and approach requires humility from an ex-majority community, which also needs to resist the opposite temptation of withdrawing into isolation and abandoning any responsibility for participating in wider social, political, economic and cultural debates and initiatives. Eric Zander, who has pioneered L'Autre Rive, an 'alternative church' in the Belgian town of Gembloux, warns: 'Churches on the margins . . . tend to protect their identity from the negative influence of "the world" by secluding themselves from the secular dominant society and developing their own microcosmic culture and relationship network.'[25] Instead of 'protective seclusion', he proposes 'influential infiltration.'

A 'vast minority' has the capacity to exert considerable influence, especially in a society that has no compelling vision to inspire it, exhibits widespread disdain for its political leadership, suspects that its economic system is broken beyond repair, is torn between arid secularism and often vapid forms of spirituality, swings wildly between relativism and judgementalism when confronted with moral dilemmas, is obsessed by trivia, toys and

---

[25] In Ryan Bolger, ed., *The Gospel after Christendom* (Grand Rapids: Baker, 2012), p. 77.

celebrity culture, and is 'amusing itself to death'.[26] But the Christian community can only rise to this challenge if we whole-heartedly embrace our minority status and learn to operate as a creative and prophetic minority.

What does this mean in practice?

- Recognizing how unappealing and unchristian are traits such as self-righteousness, smugness and moral superiority, patronizing remarks, unwillingness to listen to the views of others, hectoring, grumbling and complaining, expecting deference, and defending our own interests. And renouncing these behaviours.
- Listening attentively and empathetically, researching issues carefully, speaking with clarity and conviction but also with grace, humility and sensitivity, so that our tone is inviting and engaging, rather than overbearing.
- Appreciating the importance of modelling within the Christian community what we commend to others, so that we can speak with integrity. This does not require us to achieve perfection, nor is this so that we can claim the moral high ground, but we do need to live out authentically what we invite others to consider.
- Acknowledging the failures and shortcomings of the Christian community, past and present, and admitting that on some issues we have dragged our heels. For example, if we are to participate in efforts to refocus our society on the challenges associated with the ecological crisis, we will first confess our complicity in historic and current practices that have caused and exacerbate this crisis, and our reluctance to engage with this issue. Then we will learn, humbly and gratefully, from social movements such as the Transition Network, which not only offers resources and support to those who are encouraging local community resilience but also models a less institutionalized approach that may be more appropriate for a minority community.[27] We may in time have distinctive contributions to make and some creative alternatives to offer, rooted in different philosophical and theological presuppositions, but we cannot pretend to be pioneers in this area.

---

[26] A phrase popularized by Neil Postman, *Amusing Ourselves to Death* (York: Methuen, 1987).

[27] See http://www.transitionnetwork.org.

- Being patient and not expecting what we say and do to be respected immediately or valued highly until our society is persuaded that we are now operating from within a different paradigm and has begun to trust the Christian community and welcome our contributions.

Patience may not be an easy virtue to embrace in a Christian community anxious about its continuing decline and marginalization and worried about its future prospects. But this was what Jeremiah urged the exiles in Babylon to practise: trust in God's good purposes and do not try to force the pace. Unrealistic expectations, hyperactivity and pressure to achieve are unhelpful and counterproductive. With reference to Israel's exile experience, Nigel Wright writes:

> Several times over my years of ministry great excitement has been generated by predictions that revival is almost upon us . . . In the light of this it actually takes a certain kind of moral courage to say that perhaps these things are not going to happen . . . For the time being the wider culture appears, either deliberately or by default, largely to have decided against Christianity. Until that shifts significantly, the Western church, not by any means for the first time in its history, is likely to be in endurance mode rather than in resurgence.[28]

This does not consign the Christian community to defeatism or inaction, any more than Jeremiah was recommending this to the exiles, but 'progress is likely to be seen in the small things rather than in the greater'.[29] Wright concludes: 'We require resilience and a long term perspective concerning God's plan. The church should be seen not so much as a triumphant army taking on the host of wickedness, but as clusters of partisans steadily and creatively undermining the system for the glory of God.'[30]

This applies not only to the prophetic role of a minority Christian community but also to its evangelistic role in a society that is

---

[28] Nigel Wright, *New Baptists, New Agenda* (Carlisle: Paternoster, 2002), p. 32.

[29] Wright, *New Baptists*, p. 34.

[30] Wright, *New Baptists*, pp. 44–5.

increasingly unfamiliar with the biblical narrative, wary of religion in general and Christianity in particular, and deeply suspicious of proselytizing. In the same way that we can learn from the 'Slow Food' movement how to sustain ourselves as disciples (as was suggested in Chapter 4), so Michael Frost suggests we should practise 'slow evangelism'. He advocates a patient, incarnational approach, counteracting the abuses of fast evangelism and writes: 'We will find that evangelism is best done slowly, deliberately, in the context of a loving community. It takes time and multiple engagements.'[31] It also involves the Christian community, as individuals and together, demonstrating the gospel we proclaim and living in ways that provoke questions.[32]

Patient evangelism requires at least as much listening as speaking, creative contextualization of the gospel and, if Jesus is our model, more provocative questions than definitive answers and plenty of 'what if?' stories. Evangelism is popularly associated with arrogance, assertion and imposing views, but patient evangelism is humble. Bryan Stone, professor of evangelism at Boston University, writes: 'While humility is a perennial virtue required of evangelistic practice, it has never been more important than now for those of us who live in societies where the church is still coping with the loss of Christendom privileges and our consignment to the fringes of cultural and political significance.'[33]

Patient evangelism may also involve two-way learning, as Peter found in his encounter with Cornelius[34] – a very different scenario from proselytizing and theological imperialism. Steven Croft, currently bishop of Sheffield and formerly team leader of Fresh Expressions, asks: 'Do we believe that we are better than those around us? Do we believe that God is at work only inside the Church?' He identifies three levels of listening, advocating the third level: 'I listen in order to gain the right to speak; I listen in order to tailor my message to what you say; I listen in order

---

[31] Frost, *Road to Missional*, p. 44.

[32] One of the most helpful books on evangelism remains Graham Tomlin, *The Provocative Church* (London: SPCK, 2013), now in its third edition.

[33] Bryan Stone, *Evangelism after Christendom: The Theology and Practice of Christian Witness* (Grand Rapids: Brazos, 2007), p. 305.

[34] Acts 10, especially v. 34.

to learn from your wisdom and insight.'[35] This approach, which recognizes that God goes ahead of us and invites us to receive from others as well as sharing good news with them, is an expression of our commitment to and confidence in *missio Dei*.

Partnerships

A prophetic minority is not absorbed and domesticated by the surrounding culture but neither does it dissent from every aspect of this culture. It may understand its vocation primarily as a 'contrast society' or counter-culture, but there are some necessary caveats to this position. An obvious one in a diverse society made up of many subcultures is the complexity of working out what it means to be counter-cultural. Where does the Christian community position itself among the many minority communities that in different ways are counter-cultural in relation to whatever is perceived to be the dominant culture? With which does it make common cause and from which does it distance itself, ideologically if not relationally? Another caveat is that a prophetic minority is mandated to 'seek the welfare' of its society, which surely implies that its role might be supportive, creative and transformational, not just oppositional.

Previous chapters have advocated learning from the experience of other minorities and doing theology in conversation with other faith communities. But we can go further. In a society that homogenizes and marginalizes religious convictions and experiences, faith communities can support each other in disturbing the supposed secular consensus, challenging the notion that all religions are much the same as each other, and demonstrating the potential of united action in addressing social problems, especially in the most deprived neighbourhoods of our cities. Partnership does not involve unconditional endorsement of each other's beliefs, but it does require mutual respect. Relationships of trust and friendship across cultural and religious boundaries are a prophetic anticipation of reconciled humanity, a powerful witness against those who refuse to tolerate otherness, and a secure foundation for 'slow evangelism' that is open to receiving as well as giving.

[35] Steven Croft et al., *Evangelism in a Spiritual Age* (London: Church House Publishing, 2005), pp. 133–4.

As a minority, the Christian community can become more sensitive to the insecurities, fears and anxieties of other minorities. As a vast minority, it can mobilize its resources to support and defend their interests. Rather than bristling and protesting when its own sensibilities are offended or its own interests are threatened, the Christian community might choose to accept mistreatment and misrepresentation, swinging into action instead when other minorities are badly treated or unfairly caricatured. Rather than lobbying for influence or expecting special treatment, we might advocate for the equitable treatment of all and campaign for the removal of privileges inherited from our previous majority status.

Partnerships with government agencies, statutory bodies and other organizations are fraught with difficulties, with suspicion on both sides. The motivation of the Christian community is often questioned, for understandable reasons given our track record. During the Christendom era the church had a holistic vision and understood its vocation to include economic, political, cultural and social engagement as well as caring for the spiritual needs of the community. For hundreds of years it developed all kinds of innovative strategies, programmes and institutions at local, regional, national and transnational levels. It founded schools and universities, built hospitals and orphanages, sponsored the arts, provided charity for the destitute, and inspired movements that abolished slavery, established trade unions, improved working conditions and laid the foundations for democracy. European society is founded on Christian values and served by institutions that owe their origins to the church. But for hundreds of years it was also patronizing and overbearing, excessively wealthy and self-indulgent, frequently corrupt, prone to violently suppressing dissent, grasping after power and influence, in multiple ways betraying its founding vision and ignoring the teachings of Jesus. No wonder there is a legacy of distrust and suspicion when the church gets involved in initiatives today, either offering to partner with others or suggesting new possibilities.

But the Christian community will also be wary of being co-opted by a neo-liberal capitalist ideology, used as a cheap alternative to statutory provision, or required to disavow the faith basis that motivates our activities. In a culture of indebtedness, austerity and swingeing cuts to social welfare, the state is desperate for the church to get more involved again. There is a new recognition of the resources the church offers, especially at a local level, with its deeply committed personnel, multipurpose buildings, local knowledge and networks. The churches can deliver what is needed more effectively and at lower cost than the state can. Responding to a dramatic increase in food poverty, the Christian community has demonstrated through the Foodbanks initiative its capacity as a vast minority to respond with compassion, energy and creativity.[36] This is a widely publicized example of a renewed commitment to holistic ministry within the Christian community. Christian social entrepreneurs are initiating many new projects and programmes. But these initiatives must be combined with greater concern about challenging injustice and preventing further victimization, rather than just caring for the casualties – a prophetic challenge to politicians who are responsible for oppressive and unjust policies and to a wealthy society that tolerates such poverty.

Partnership will require churches and other agencies to move beyond suspicion, build trust and be open about their agendas. This will mean other agencies recognizing that Christians are motivated by our faith, not expecting us to hide or apologize for this, and accepting that this does not mean we will use our activities as a cover for proselytizing. It will mean them acknowledging that the long-term presence of Christians in marginal communities gives us credibility and crucial insights. And it will mean them not being surprised or offended if we pose awkward questions about strategies, the allocation of resources, injustices, or the scope of initiatives. But all of this is predicated on the Christian community demonstrating clearly and consistently that it has renounced past compromises, is committed to unconditional and transparent social engagement, understands its changed role as a minority in a plural society, and is whole-heartedly embracing partnership.

And as a minority, the Christian community will need to make hard choices about where and how to deploy its limited resources, guided by the potential to make a creative and prophetic contribution. Taking on too much will exhaust us and diminish our impact. But the Christian community is a vast minority. It has

---

[36] See http://www.trusselltrust.org/foodbank-projects for details of the Christian charity behind many Foodbanks.

resources, personnel, expertise, relationships and historic rooted-
ness, especially within local neighbourhoods, beyond that of any
other organization. In the past we have often acted unilaterally
or insisted on maintaining control of our initiatives, which has
limited our effectiveness and opportunities to share faith with
others in the context of shared activities. Partnering with others is
more appropriate for a minority community, and taking initiatives
that we help to catalyse but need not dominate or control releases
energy for fresh initiatives. Working with and alongside others,
rather than doing things for them, is not only more respectful of
their skills, experience and gifts and more effective in the long
run. It also transforms the 'power relations' and offers a much
more conducive context for exploring issues of faith and discipleship.

Partnership involves recognition both of common goals and
the distinctive contribution each partner can make. In a social
context in which local community has often become fragmented
and neighbourliness has diminished, the churches may have
limited resources but may still have a greater capacity than any
other group or organization to respond to this challenge and
form alliances with others to rebuild and nurture neighbourhoods that are more integrated and more conducive to human
flourishing. Eddie Gibbs writes: 'Churches, working alongside other locally grounded groups, have the potential to make
a significant contribution to the realization of [communities
made up of people who know and care about one another].' He
concludes: 'The church must work alongside other faith-based
groups and whoever shares the vision of replacing an individualistic and consumerist society with one that develops networks
of relationships.'[37]

Baptist minister Simon Jones is convinced that opportunities
for creative partnerships should be taken and that the Christian
community has much to offer that others will soon learn to value.
He writes: 'Working with others – churches, voluntary organizations, the statutory sector – means that genuine partnerships are
formed and genuinely new services can be created out of those
partnerships. We bring our skills, insights, contacts, workforce

---

[37] Eddie Gibbs, *The Rebirth of the Church* (Grand Rapids: Baker, 2013), p.
250.

to the table and can quickly establish ourselves as equals in the provision of a range of services.'[38]

From beyond the churches, too, come suggestions that a minority Christian community can make significant contributions – and that these will be welcomed. A striking example appears in '50 Things that Will Save the Planet', an Environment Agency document reporting on the views of twenty-five experts invited to nominate their top five recommendations. At number 2 is the role the Christian community and other faith communities might play in saving the planet. Chris Goodall wrote: 'They need to form a coalition to encourage their followers to set an example to the rest of the population.' And Nick Reeves agreed: 'It is time that they fulfilled their rightful collective role in reminding us that we have a duty to restore and maintain the ecological balance of the planet.'[39]

Contributors to *Working Faith: Faith-Based Organizations and Urban Social Justice* also encourage the Christian community to enter into 'post-secular partnerships', but suggest we should fill gaps under protest, resist co-option and exercise a prophetic role within these partnerships.

> Meeting unmet need is an ethical imperative; however, filling the gap is a deeply ambiguous political position. At times it can be seen as a powerful form of political protest to achieve change, and at other times it can be regarded as a placatory device that justifies state retrenchment in direct provision. Faith involvement that identifies itself purely as a social service provider runs the risk of losing sight of the church's prophetic role to redeem the 'powers that be' and address the uncomfortable questions about why people live highly precarious lives.[40]

---

[38] Roger Standing, *As a Fire by Burning* (London: SCM Press, 2013), p. 54.

[39] Nick Reeves, *Your Environment Extra 17* (November 2007–January 2008), p. 16.

[40] Maarten Davelaar, Andrew Williams and Justin Beaumont, 'Adventures at a Border Crossing: Society for Diaconal Social Work in Rotterdam, The Netherlands', in *Working Faith: Faith-Based Organizations and Urban Social Justice* (ed. Paul Cloke, Justin Beaumont and Andrew Williams; Milton Keynes: Paternoster, 2013), p. 182.

Another dimension of partnership with disturbing prophetic potential involves us recognizing the significance of being members of a transnational, multicultural community. According to the New Testament, this global community takes priority over national loyalties, for we are members of the body of Christ and only 'resident aliens' in the various nations in which we live. And the visions of Isaiah look forward to the end of warfare and the reconciliation of all nations. This perspective was difficult to maintain when the interests of a dominant Christian majority were hard to disentangle from the interests of the nation in which it was located and which looked to it for support and legitimation. Members of the global Christian community fought and killed one another as they placed loyalty to nation above loyalty to Christ and his community. Alan Kreider offers a sobering example: the nuclear bomb that in 1945 destroyed Nagasaki 'was dropped by a US plane, piloted by Catholic crewmen who were given spiritual support by Catholic padres, upon a target whose epicentre was a Roman Catholic cathedral at the heart of the largest Christian community in Japan; the bomb wiped out two orders of Catholic nuns'.[41]

A minority Christian community has an opportunity, and responsibility, to repent of this misplaced allegiance and to insist that 'national self-interest' does not trump loyalty to the global Christian community. This phrase, beloved by politicians, is meant to persuade the electorate that our interests are being prioritized and defended. But unrestrained self-seeking is no more moral at a national level than at a personal level. This is a pernicious and myopic doctrine. For leaders of a wealthy nation like Britain to base policies on national self-interest rather than on justice for the global community and peaceful cooperation between nations is ethically indefensible, but this is worn as a badge of pride. A minority Christian community that prioritizes its relationship with the global Christian community will refuse to endorse such narrow nationalism.

An encouraging statement of intent was the Berlin Declaration, issued in May 2001 by the Baptist World Alliance, which confessed past complicity and recognized that 'nationalism or adherence to

---

[41] Alan and Eleanor Kreider, *Becoming a Peace Church* (London: London Mennonite Centre, 2000), p. 37.

a national ideology which exalts one nation over others are forms of idolatry and not compatible with Christian beliefs'.[42] This is a strong statement and was accompanied by a commitment to oppose war as a way of settling disputes between nations and to work for justice and peace. It represents a determination to orientate our priorities towards the vision Isaiah saw and to align ourselves with the fulfilment of God's mission.

Taking such a stance will be unpopular, however, especially when war is threatened or fear of terrorism is high. Members of the Muslim community are frequently accused of placing their allegiance to the global Muslim community above that of loyalty to Britain. If the Christian community adopts a similar stance and declares openly where its primary allegiance lies, the powerful idolatry of nationalism might be laid bare.

However, on this and so many other issues, the capacity of the Christian community as a vast minority to speak and act prophetically is undermined by our disunity. We cannot revel in the possibilities of partnering with others without acknowledging this debilitating reality. During the past fifteen years I have had the privilege of working as a trainer and mission consultant with over thirty denominations and many Christian organizations. Despite different histories, theologies, structures and terminology, they have far more in common than divides them and all are facing very similar challenges and opportunities.[43]

Old-style ecumenism that operates from the top down through commissions, committees, statements and conferences has run out of steam. Indeed, Richard Koenig predicted forty years ago: 'If there is an impulse toward unity, it will come from local or regional rather than national centers and spring from the demands of mission and perceived theological consensus rather than denominational decree . . . The place where the creativity of the minority has to be most

---

[42] The full text can be found at http://www.bpnews.net/bpnews. asp?ID=11040.

[43] Although there are also different challenges facing national churches and the so-called 'Free Churches'. The former will need to renounce what an Anglican friend refers to as their 'effortless superiority' in their attitudes towards other parts of the Christian community. The latter will need to move beyond a dissenting stance that defines them over against other parts of the Christian community.

in evidence is the congregation.'[44] And there is mounting evidence of a new grass-roots missional ecumenism in many places, which will thrive if it receives gentle encouragement. Perhaps, in time, a minority Christian community will be sufficiently coherent to speak with a united voice. Until then, as suggested in an earlier chapter, local credibility may be more important than official pronouncements or programmes.

---

[44] Richard Koenig, *A Creative Minority: The Church in a New Age* (Minneapolis: Augsburg, 1971), pp. 72 and 106.

7.

A Hopeful Minority

Hope

A prophetic minority will frequently ask the 'what if?' question we introduced in the previous chapter. What if we renounced the use of violence and invested massively in peace-building initiatives? What if, despite its grievous failures to live out the gospel, the story the church has carried through the centuries is actually true? What if the resources of our remarkably affluent society were distributed more equally so that many social welfare initiatives became redundant? What if nationalism is idolatrous in many instances and patriotism needs to be integrated with global concern? What if we moved beyond oppositional debates characterized by misinformation, caricature and desperation to win arguments, and learned to engage in humble, patient and open conversations?

Asking 'what if?' engages the imagination and, like good stories, this opens up conversations rather than closing them down. It invites exploration of alternative possibilities. In a word, it engenders hope.

Contemporary Western societies are not awash with hope. The culture of modernity that was shaped by the Enlightenment was optimistic about future prospects in ways that we now find naïve and difficult to imagine. Expectations were high that rationalism, scientific discoveries, technological advances and political initiatives would make the twentieth century a golden age of peace and prosperity. In stark contrast, the years leading up to the dawn of the twenty-first century were marked by distrust of technology (do you remember the 'millennium bug'?), disengagement from politics, scepticism and anxiety as post-modernity dismantled the certainties of modernity and inculcated a mood of increasing pessimism. But neither optimism nor pessimism should be equated with hope.

A prophetic minority is energized and sustained by hope. A community that takes its bearings from *missio Dei* and anticipates the earth filled with *shalom* and the knowledge of God need not swing wildly between optimism and pessimism. Hope is related to God's ultimate purposes for humanity and the cosmos (eschatology in theological terms) rather than short-term expectations. And our hope is rooted in the resurrection. Lesslie Newbigin responded to questions asking if he was optimistic or pessimistic about the future of the church in India by saying, 'I believe that Jesus rose from the dead, and therefore the question does not arise.'[1] And John Howard Yoder claimed that, uniquely, the hope of the Christian community does not depend on being in charge or taking control of the political process to restructure society but on our conviction that Jesus, the slain lamb, is Lord. The way of Christ, culminating in the cross and resurrection, is the model of Christian social efficacy and transformation.[2]

This has implications for the Christian community itself and for its witness. Earlier chapters asked what expectations a declining minority Christian community that used to be a majority might realistically have in relation to its own survival or possible flourishing in Britain and other Western societies. We noted divergent narratives of decline and growth and suggested that continuing, if decelerating, decline might be punctuated and at some point reversed by examples of growth. Neither pessimism nor optimism are helpful responses. Pessimism and discouragement are powerful temptations for an ex-majority community facing uncertainty in the face of declining numbers and influence. Optimistic predictions of revival and seizing on any indications of renewed growth are understandable but unhelpful reactions.

If the analogy with the exile in Babylon, to which we and others have had frequent recourse, is trustworthy, we might heed Jeremiah's counsel and concentrate on modest but essential activities: disavowing past compromises; forming and sustaining resilient

---

[1] Quoted in Peter McDowell, *At Home in Exile* (Belfast: Contemporary Christianity, 2012), p. 68.

[2] Yoder, as summarized in Earl Zimmerman, *Practicing the Politics of Jesus* (Telford, PA: Cascadia, 2007), pp, 192–3.

communities; learning to 'sing the Lord's song in a strange land'; sowing seeds rather than anticipating an imminent harvest; accepting our current status as both judgement and liberation; and trusting God for a future that we can no longer pretend to control.

But the most challenging aspect of Jeremiah's letter was his insistence that the welfare of the exiles was inextricably linked with the welfare of the society in which they now lived: 'seek the *shalom* of the city . . . in its *shalom* you will find your *shalom*.' A minority community can become fixated on its own prospects and fail to empathize or engage with the loss of hope in society. Michael Frost asks those obsessed with changing their churches: 'What if we spent as much time obsessing about how to change our world, our city, or our neighbourhood?'[3]

Engendering hope might be one of the most potent contributions of a prophetic minority. And this will require the Christian community to embody, patiently and humbly, different reflexes and responses. Maybe this is what Jesus envisaged when he compared the kingdom of God to the actions of yeast and salt.[4] A small amount of yeast, hidden in the dough and disappearing as the bread rises, is unheralded but transformative. Salt has many purposes and Jesus' words can be interpreted in various ways. A pinch of salt flavours bland food and can preserve meat that would otherwise rot. But when Jesus tells his disciples they are the 'salt of the earth' (or ground), he might be referring to its use as a fertilizer – a more proactive and creative image.

What might be involved in engendering hope? What counter-cultural responses might point to a different perspective on the present and the future? Two examples will have to suffice here.

Stability

A society that lacks hope is constantly tinkering, rebuilding, rebranding and upgrading. It is characterized by impatience, short-termism, built-in obsolescence and the demand for instant gratification. Projects, programmes and initiatives follow each other in rapid succession, abandoned before they can take effect

---

[3] Michael Frost, *The Road to Missional* (Grand Rapids: Baker, 2011), p. 103.

[4] See Matt 13:33; 5:13.

properly, resulting in instability, anxiety and wasted resources – as teachers and those who work in the health service know all too well. No wonder there is so much scepticism and disengagement! And the Christian community is not immune to this, as churches hop from one strategy to another, as church members move from church to church, and as funders withdraw support if results are not achieved quickly. But a hopeful minority can embody stability. It can stay in particular places and journey with communities for years and decades as initiatives come and go.

Once again, Jeremiah's counsel to the exiles resonates with what some are advocating today. Australian mission educators Kim Hammond and Darren Cronshaw include 'shalom spirituality' as one of six 'postures of missional Christians' and commend stability as one aspect of this. Quoting Jeremiah 29, they note the importance attached to the exiles settling, physically and emotionally, and putting down deep roots.[5] And Eddie Gibbs urges the abandonment of relationships that are 'casual' (shallow and peripheral) or 'contractual' (broken off when someone becomes dissatisfied) and the adoption of 'covenantal' relationships in the Christian community – relationships that persist despite stresses and discouragements.[6]

Christians in poor urban neighbourhoods more often demonstrate this stability than those in more affluent and mobile areas. This week I heard of a young couple who had moved into a poor urban neighbourhood with a commitment to be there for at least the next thirty years. An Anglican friend describes the vocation of his urban congregation as 'outlasting, out-praying and, if necessary, out-suffering' all who hinder or oppose the advance of God's mission in their community. And many small urban churches provide a simple but powerful testimony to hope simply by still being there.[7]

---

5 Kim Hammond and Darren Cronshaw, *Sentness: Six Postures of Missional Christians* (Downers Grove: IVP, 2014), pp. 97–8.

6 Eddie Gibbs, *The Rebirth of the Church* (Grand Rapids: Baker, 2013), p. 148.

7 See further Jonathan Wilson-Hartgrove, *The Wisdom of Stability: Rooting Faith in a Mobile Culture* (Brewster, MA: Paraclete Press, 2010); and the chapter on stability in C. Christopher Smith and John Pattison, *Slow Church: Cultivating Community in the Patient Way of Jesus* (Downers Grove: IVP, 2014), pp. 59–78.

Gratitude

A society that lacks hope is characterized by complaining, grumbling, cynicism, anxiety and finding fault. This is evident in day-to-day encounters and conversations: listen to the tone of queues in supermarkets and at bus stops. It is apparent in the 'blame culture' that goes well beyond requiring people to take responsibility and hunts for scapegoats whenever anything goes wrong. It characterizes many of our neighbourhoods with many afraid to go out, afraid to answer the door, afraid of strangers, afraid to get involved with others, resulting in great loneliness. It reveals itself in passivity, scepticism and reluctance to join campaigning organizations, political parties, pressure groups, or even to vote in a system widely viewed as discredited. It dominates the news media, which not only present a skewed view of the world in their unrelenting coverage of 'bad news' stories but, when they do report on constructive ideas and hopeful initiatives, also hunt for critics to interview in order to reveal flaws.

Film critic Gareth Higgins deplores the malign impact this media coverage has on society, although he acknowledges that the media reflect the society they serve. This was evident in a recent experiment carried out by a Russian newspaper. The *City Reporter* in Rostov-on-Don decided to publish only good news for one day. Its website had asked on the previous day: 'Do you feel like you are surrounded by negative information? Do you think good news is a myth? We'll try to prove the opposite tomorrow!' On 1 December 2014, as promised, the website carried only positive headlines. But these good news stories sent readership numbers plummeting: the website lost two-thirds of its readers that day.[8]

Recalling his own journalistic experience, Higgins writes, 'We looked for the conflict angle on every story.' But unremitting reporting of violence, crises, threats and disasters breeds fear, desensitizes society, distorts reality and offers no hope. He concludes: 'The way you tell the story about your world will actually co-create that world. The myth of redemptive violence needs to be replaced. It is up to us to invent a new myth.'[9]

---

[8] See http: // www.bbc.co.uk / news / blogs-news-from-elsewhere-30318261.

[9] Gareth Higgins, 'Here Isn't the News'. *Third Way* 37/7 (2014), pp. 9–12.

And we have a new 'myth', the promise of the New Jerusalem into which the treasures of the nations will be brought.[10] Although the city descends from heaven as the gift of God – for we cannot establish it ourselves – we can rejoice that the noblest of human accomplishments will find their place in the city. And we can be grateful for every creative initiative, every act of kindness, every expression of generosity, every bold experiment that anticipates the *shalom*-filled future God has promised and points hopefully towards this. We will not close our eyes to the evil all around and within us, nor will we cease to rage against injustice, but we can choose to redress the balance in a complaining culture by being grateful.

An amusing but powerful example of subverting the news media's negativity and challenging perceptions of reality was reported in a TED talk by Kelli Anderson.[11] Her team managed to produce and distribute hundreds of thousands of copies of a counterfeit *New York Times* and filmed the reactions of unsuspecting readers confronted by 'good news' headlines instead of the doom and gloom they were expecting. This fake but convincing issue, which was dated six months in the future, replaced the regular slogan 'all the news that's fit to print' with 'all the news we hope to print' and invited readers to imagine a different world that was more just and more peaceful. This presentation is well worth watching, not least for the dumbfounded expressions on the faces of those who read the headlines and stare in disbelief! The vocation of the Christian community as a prophetic minority is, similarly, to subvert the dominant narrative and point towards a different future that engages the imagination and engenders hope.

A more poignant example of offering a different perspective on a situation dominating the news headlines appeared as I was revising this chapter. It is worth quoting at length, not least because it picks up the theme of hope and what we might learn from the prophetic witness of another minority Christian community.

Elie Haddad, president of the Arab Baptist Theological Seminary in Beirut, reports on a gathering at which Christian leaders from various Middle Eastern countries shared news of the tragic events affecting their region. However, he writes:

[10] Rev. 21:24–6.
[11] See http://www.ted.com/talks/kelli_anderson_design_to_challenge_reality.

We also heard another side of the story, a story that is not told by the news media. A story of God at work in the middle of all the tragedies. A story about churches being transformed by the dreadful situation around them, moving from a survival-mode attitude to a community of God's people that has a loud and clear prophetic voice, churches that are discovering how to be agents of hope in the middle of hopelessness around them and agents of reconciliation despite the violence surrounding them. A story about people of different faiths and backgrounds encountering the Gospel for the first time in their lives through the church communities that are caring for them holistically . . . As Christians and the Church are progressively losing power, we are discovering that the call of Jesus works best through powerlessness . . . The Church is being transformed in our region as it wrestles with what it means to carry on ministry from the margin through powerlessness.[12]

Courage

Subverting the dominant narrative, challenging assumptions, questioning priorities and exposing idolatry might align us with other minorities in our society but this will not endear us to the powerful defenders of the status quo or those whose economic interests are at stake. If our vocation is to be a prophetic minority, rather than a compliant or isolationist minority, might we eventually discomfort the 'powers that be' enough that we face opposition or even suffering? This is the classic response to prophetic provocation.

There is little immediate prospect of this. And we should not confuse this possibility with the very minor forms of discrimination that some ludicrously regard as persecution, antagonism provoked by Christians speaking arrogantly or behaving stupidly, or unease that the Christian community is no longer privileged or protected as it once was. But if we embrace the call to be a prophetic minority, and especially if we challenge our society in the areas of provision, protection and the 'national interest', things might change quite rapidly. After all, we are a vast minority with considerable influence if we choose to use this.

---

[12] Writing in the Arab Baptist Theological Seminary newsletter (October 2014), pp. 1–2.

Eddie Gibbs writes: 'Churches seeking to bear witness to the gospel in the pluralistic West are likely to meet with increasing suspicion, misrepresentation, and hostility . . . If and when hostility increases, Christians must ensure that they bear witness with bold-ness and grace, remembering Jesus' exhortation to love our enemies.' Of course, this depends on how we understand the gospel: a privat-ized and spiritualized gospel is unlikely to give offence. Nor are generalized statements in support of social justice, creation care or the relief of poverty. But if we challenge ultimate loyalties and expose the idols of militarism and consumerism, there may well be a backlash. In which case, Gibbs continues, we 'need to rediscover a theology of suffering, and we need to do so without developing a persecution complex'.[13] After all, there are many indications in the New Testament that faithful discipleship and prophetic testimony will result in suffering.[14]

This is another aspect of discipleship on which we can learn from minorities in other times and places that have experienced discrimination, victimization and marginalization in line with biblical expectations. A community faces different challenges when it enjoys majority or minority status. Ralph Sockman, American pastor and broadcaster, famously commented: 'The test of toler-ance comes when we are in a majority; the test of courage comes when we are in a minority.' The Christian community sadly failed the test of tolerance when we were a majority community. Perhaps this period of exile is an opportunity to repent whole-heartedly of our oppression of minorities and commit ourselves never to repeat this behaviour if we again become a majority community.

We may also at some point in Western societies face the test of courage. It took courage to be a follower of Jesus in the minority Christian communities of the first three centuries. It took no courage to be a Christian in Christendom, unless you dissented from what were regarded as orthodox views. In fact, it took courage *not* to be a Christian. In many parts of the world today – not least in the countries of the Middle East to which Elie Haddad refers – it takes great courage to be a Christian and to respond prophetically and hopefully to provocation and persecution. But in post-Christendom Western societies it takes only a little courage

[13] Gibbs, *Rebirth of the Church*, p. 218.
[14] For example, Matt. 5:10–12; 2 Tim. 3:12 and 1 Pet. 2:20–25.

at present to be known as a follower of Jesus. This may not always be so.

We are rightly concerned for our brothers and sisters in this region, but we must also heed their counsel as they explain how we can support them. Haddad concludes:

> We are grateful for the way the global Church is supporting us and empowering us . . . However, our invitation to the Western Church today should not be to come and save us, or to come and protect us. We are not victims. We are not looking for a new 'Christendom' in our region or for a new wave of military crusaders. Our invitation for the global Church today is to come and join us. Join us in proclaiming the love of Jesus to everyone in the region, to our friends and to our enemies.

Impact

What impact might a minority Christian community have? Enough to bring down serious opposition on our heads? Enough to offer a compelling alternative narrative in a culture that seems to be devoid of this?

The failures, abuses and compromises of the Christendom era are well known and frequently rehearsed. An ex-majority Christian community will continue to grieve and disavow these if it is to have any credibility today. But a prophetic minority might also, humbly and without expecting a ready response, encourage a culture with no compelling alternative narrative to reconsider the Christian story, its values and priorities, and its legacy in Western societies. It is possible to celebrate and commend the remarkable achievements of Christendom without whitewashing this era. And it is legitimate to ask what has been lost and for how much longer a post-Christendom culture can live off this legacy while undermining its foundations. So we will weigh carefully the views of various writers as they reassess the Christendom legacy and reflect on contributions a minority Christian community might yet make in Western societies.

Tom Wright, former bishop of Durham and prolific New Testament scholar, presents a more sanguine evaluation of the Christendom era than many would endorse, but he rightly points out that both sides of the story need to be told:

The failure of Christianity is a modern myth, and we shouldn't be ashamed of telling the proper story of church history, which of course has plenty of muddle and wickedness, but also far more than we normally imagine of love and creativity and beauty and justice and healing and education and hope. To imagine the world without the gospel of Jesus is to imagine a pretty bleak place.[15]

Elsewhere he writes:

We live at a time of cultural crisis. At the moment I don't find anyone out there pointing a way forward out of the postmodern morass; some people are still trying to put up the shutters and live in a pre-modern world, many are clinging to modernism for all they're worth, and many are deciding that living off the pickings of the garbage-heap of postmodernity is the best option on offer. But we can do better than that . . . The gospel of Jesus points us, and indeed urges us, to be at the leading edge of the whole culture, articulating . . . worldview which will mount the historically rooted Christian challenge to both modernity and postmodernity, leading the way into the post-postmodern world with joy and humour and gentleness and good judgement and true wisdom.[16]

Christopher Marshall, professor of restorative justice at Victoria University of Wellington, also celebrates the accomplishments of Christendom, despite its many failures:

From its very inception the church developed a system of social assistance that no civic or religious office in the pagan world had ever provided. After Constantine, the church became the first organized institution of large-scale public welfare in Western history, a great repository and redistributor of goods, alms, state moneys, and bequests that funded hospitals, orphanages, hostels, and asylums. The church often failed to live up to its own compassionate ideals, as is frequently pointed out these days. But even in its failures, the church achieved far more than the Roman gods had ever inspired.[17]

---

[15] N.T. Wright, *How God Became King* (London: SPCK, 2012), p. 163.

[16] N.T. Wright, *The Challenge of Jesus* (London: SPCK, 2000), p. 151.

[17] Christopher Marshall, *Compassionate Justice* (Eugene, OR: Wipf & Stock, 2012), p. 274.

He asks:

> As the plausibility of the Christian vision of reality recedes in the West, a question mark hangs over the future of our moral culture: will its 'gentler ethical prejudices', such as compassion for the weak and service of the indigent, persist once the faith that gave them meaning has withered away? . . . As the Christian rationale for love's supremacy ceases to be self-evident to our society, only time will tell whether the compassionate habits it has fostered will retain their grip for long on our collective hearts and minds.[18]

Another who enumerates some of the contributions made to European society by those who believed the Christian narrative is Jeff Fountain, although he suggests that these were often the efforts of minority communities, rather than the majority Christian community. He writes:

> Minorities faithful to Jesus' teachings have played a totally disproportionate role in Europe's welfare. Despite many dark chapters of church history, when believers were faithful to Christ's character, movements began that liberated slaves, emancipated women, alleviated suffering, championed justice, cared for the sick and sheltered refugees. Creative Christian minorities in modern times initiated the Red Cross, the SPCA, Alcoholics Anonymous, Amnesty International, cooperative banks and countless NGO's. Even the story of the European Union begins with devout believers like Robert Schuman and Konrad Adenauer who set out to obey Christ's command to love one's neighbour in international politics, believing that Europe's only hope was to be rebuilt on Christian foundations.[19]

Minority Christian communities in Britain also made significant contributions to the welfare of society, despite having limited political influence and being barred from the universities and therefore from professions that required university education. A well-known nineteenth-century example is the development of Bournville, in Birmingham, by the wealthy Quaker factory

---

[18] Marshall, *Compassionate Justice*, p. 258.

[19] Writing in *Vista* 14 (2013): pp. 2–3.

owner, George Cadbury. This creative and prophetic development set new standards in the provision of good housing with gardens, a healthy environment and leisure facilities for factory workers. Congregationalists, Unitarians and Baptists were also involved in campaigns against the slave trade, gambling and alcoholism, the provision of Sunday schools, support for the emerging trade unions and various attempts to ameliorate the appalling conditions of those who worked in industry. Some of these initiatives involved political action as well as grass-roots activities, and all required a vision for social transformation beyond the walls of their local congregations, but none of them required majority status or implied acceptance of the ideology of Christendom.

Nigel Wright concludes:

> Christendom's vision of society has its own coherence and has left its mark in myriad ways on the architecture, the culture and the governmental systems of the world. It provided a unified and integrated vision of life, a social harmony in which all aspects of human experience could be integrated and cared for. It offered a sacred canopy within which life could be lived out. It is not surprising that some mourn its loss or fantasize about its recovery. It was not all bad and when compared with its alternatives or replacements there is much that could be said in favour of it. But the fact is that it has been lost and will never be recovered.[20]

Any attempt to commend the Christian story and its historical outworkings must, of course, not only anticipate significant resistance and no little antipathy but also be dissociated from any suggestion that Christendom should be restored. It will be the acknowledged weakness of the Christian community and its wholehearted renunciation of grasping after power and influence that might open up fresh opportunities to tell its story and offer hope to a disillusioned, jaded and weary culture. A hopeful minority will look forwards, not backwards, imagining and describing a different future, shaped by the Christian story in more authentic ways than in the Christendom era. And, however slowly and reluctantly, a

[20] Nigel Wright, *New Baptists, New Agenda* (Carlisle: Paternoster, 2002), pp. 96–7.

post-Christendom culture might just possibly embrace a more appreciative assessment of the Christendom legacy, welcome some of the creative contributions of a Christian community and, in the absence of any compelling alternative narrative, begin to pay attention once more to the Christian story. This story might currently be believed by only a minority in British society, but the impact of a vast minority that is shaped and energized by this story might be surprising.

Vision

This is not, however, the extent of our hope or the primary focus of our vision. Whatever the prospects of the Christian community in Britain may be over the coming years, and whatever impact the Christian story might have in a post-Christendom culture, our calling is to a much broader vision and to a hope firmly rooted in God's purposes and promises.

The Christian community in Britain, as we noted previously, is not only a minority in Britain but a minority in the global Christian community. The centre of gravity of the world church is no longer in Europe or North America but in Africa, Asia and Latin America. In these regions the Christian community is growing rapidly and from these regions missionaries are coming to re-evangelize the old Christendom heartlands, re-energize discouraged congregations and plant new churches. Many more missionaries are now coming from what were once known as 'receiving nations' to the former 'sending nations' than are heading in the opposite direction. These designations are as anachronistic as the old boundaries that once divided Christendom from 'heathendom'. It is too soon to assess what impact these 'reverse mission' initiatives might make on the Christian community in Britain or on a post-Christendom culture. But the growth and multiplication of churches planted by these missionaries in London is one of the main reasons why this city is bucking the trend of decline and reporting overall growth in the Christian community.

There are challenges ahead if these missionaries and the churches they have planted are to have an impact beyond the diaspora communities in which their activities have so far been concentrated. Some of the features that make their churches so attractive within these ethnic communities unwittingly discourage others from joining them. Some of these churches have imported back to Britain beliefs, structures and practices that characterized the Christendom era and were exported as 'Christian' by Western missionaries but which are now unhelpful and inappropriate in post-Christendom Britain. Just as Western missionaries needed to learn cross-cultural mission skills (and unlearn various assumptions), so too reverse missionaries will need to make these painful adjustments. The transition from first-generation leaders to the British-born second generation will be difficult to negotiate but offers the best prospects for more effective cross-cultural engagement and the emergence of multicultural churches, especially if missional partnerships can be forged across cultural divides.

But whether the Christian community in Britain, buoyed by reverse mission, grows or not, it will remain a minority – and almost certainly a diminishing minority – within the expanding global Christian community. Several times in the past twenty centuries the centre of gravity of the Christian community has shifted to another part of the world, but it takes time for our perspectives and structures to catch up. Only slowly are Western denominations and mission agencies adjusting to this new reality, appointing leaders from non-Western nations, locating their head-quarters in the global south, developing new forms of partnership, and welcoming the insights of Asian, African and Latin American theologians and missiologists. Parochial vision continues to hinder many in the Christian community in Britain from recognizing and celebrating the dynamic growth of the global Christian community. Perhaps the prayers of British Christians for revival have been answered after all – but elsewhere rather than in our context. This is not to minimize various problematic features of this extraordinary growth in numbers and influence, especially in contexts where a vast minority might become a majority within the foreseeable future, or to deny that the experience of Western Christians might offer necessary warnings to those intent on gaining power. Philip Jenkins' survey of the emerging global Christian community, *The Next Christendom*, is exciting but salutary reading.[21] But it is to insist on a truly global vision as the context within which to understand and interpret the transition of the Christian community in Britain from majority to minority status.[22]

Expanding our vision to embrace the global Christian community and acknowledging that we are no longer at its centre is both humbling and encouraging. We are members of a truly vast minority that continues to respond, despite setbacks, unfaithfulness and distractions, to the command of the risen Jesus to take the good news of God's kingdom to the ends of the earth.

What can we expect this vast minority to achieve? What can we hope for? Optimistic and pessimistic expectations vie with each other within the complex and disputatious branch of theology known as eschatology. Advocates of each perspective present biblical evidence in support of their position. Some expect the Christian community to expand and fill the earth as the gospel is proclaimed in all nations and millions respond to this message. At the beginning of the twentieth century, delegates at mission conferences shared the optimistic outlook of the Western world and envisioned global evangelization 'in this generation'. Such a prospect may no longer seem realistic, but some are still confident that the vast minority will not always be a minority. Others recall Jesus asking, 'When the Son of Man comes, will he find faith on earth?'[23] and envision a tiny but courageous remnant waiting patiently for his return. In both camps are those who are convinced, as many previous generations have been, that Jesus will return in our generation. Others are open to the possibility that history still has thousands of years to run, with numerous twists and turns, and that we are, in effect, still in the era of the early church.

Whatever our perspective and expectations in relation to the vast minority that is the global Christian community, we are also

---

[21] Philip Jenkins, *The Next Christendom* (Oxford: Oxford University Press, 2002). Although we should heed the critique of his perspective in Jehu Hanciles, *Beyond Christendom* (Maryknoll: Orbis, 2008).

[22] Some expect India to have 126 million Christians by 2050. And, although estimates vary, the Chinese church may already number 90 million and could be 250 million by 2030, making it the largest Christian community in the world, but still a minority in China.

[23] Luke 18:8.

members of a planetary community facing what some regard as a
'perfect storm' of crises and challenges. As this chapter was being
written, fears that the Ebola virus would become a global pandemic
were subsiding, but this is only the latest in a series of health threats.
Three men accused of plotting to behead someone on the streets
of Britain were in court and authorities in several nations were
warning that terrorist attacks were inevitable as spin-offs from the
seemingly endless cycle of violence in the Middle East. The global
economy is recovering only slowly from the meltdown of 2008 and
at huge cost to the most vulnerable members of society. Further
trouble surely lies ahead for a system that is unjust and unsustainable. Overpopulation, food and water shortages, peak oil and many
other challenges rise to the top of the media agenda periodically
before subsiding once more. And the prospect of damaging or even
catastrophic climate change looms ever nearer as attention to short-
term economic and political concerns distract world leaders from
taking action. Jeremiah reminded the exiles in Babylon that their
wellbeing, their shalom, was inextricably linked with that of the
Babylonians. And Paul, in an extraordinary passage in his letter to
the Romans, insists that the future of creation itself is mysteriously
linked to the future of 'the children of God'.[24]

Our hope, therefore, cannot be limited to what the Christian
community in Britain or globally might achieve. Our vision must
embrace the purposes of God for the whole of creation. In an era
when some are frightened and tempted to despair in the face of
these threats, when others dismiss these threats, downplay their
seriousness or blithely assume technological, economic and military solutions will be found, and most ignore them because they
are preoccupied with daily concerns and regard these issues as too
big and complex to engage with, our vocation as a hopeful minority
is to live towards a different vision. We will not be immune from
anxiety, unrealistic assumptions or avoidance, but we have the
resources as we worship and reflect on the biblical story in our
communities of discernment and resistance to reject these temptations and embody our hope in the purposes and promises of God.
Inspired by the mountain visions of Isaiah, Jeremiah's assurance
of a 'future with hope',[25] John's revelation of the city of God as

[24] Rom. 8:19–21.
[25] Jer. 29:11.

humanity's new home at the centre of the new heavens and a new earth[26] and, above all, Jesus' declaration that the kingdom of God has drawn near,[27] we can celebrate every sign of the new creation, every shard of *shalom*, every inbreaking of the kingdom. We can join hands with others who are working for a more just, peaceful and sustainable world, grateful for their energy, commitment and persistence, and maybe we will offer encouragement and fresh resources to sustain hope in the face of massive challenges.

What Kind of Minority?

We return finally to the question with which we began Chapter 5. The Christian community in Britain will be, for the foreseeable future, a minority. There is no question about this. The only question is what kind of minority we will choose to be.

The transition from majority status will not be easy and many will find it disorientating and discouraging, but it is actually full of possibilities. We need not be a despondent, isolationist, grumpy or frightened minority. Nor need we become compliant and conformist, relinquishing our convictions in return for social and cultural acceptability. We can choose to interpret this emerging context as an opportunity to recover our nerve, our soul, our missional identity and our primary allegiance. We can choose to be a creative minority, a prophetic minority and a hopeful minority – a community that unmasks idols, pioneers new possibilities and engenders authentic hope. Such a minority is living towards the future that God has promised and, as a vast minority, can be a signpost pointing many others in this direction.

---

[26] Rev. 21:1–2.
[27] Mark 1:15.

Select Bibliography

Augsburger, David. *Dissident Discipleship* (Grand Rapids: Brazos, 2006).

Avis, Paul, ed. *Public Faith?* (London: SPCK, 2003).

Bolger, Ryan, ed. *The Gospel after Christendom* (Grand Rapids: Baker, 2012).

Brierley, Peter. *Capital Church Growth* (London: ADBC Publishers, 2014).

Brierley, Peter. *Pulling out of the Nosedive* (London: Christian Research, 2006).

Brierley, Peter. *The Tide is Running Out* (London: Christian Research, 2000).

Brueggemann, Walter. *The Prophetic Imagination* (Minneapolis: Fortress Press, 2001).

Cloke, Paul, Justin Beaumont and Andrew Williams, eds. *Working Faith: Faith-Based Organizations and Urban Social Justice* (Milton Keynes: Paternoster, 2013).

Davie, Grace. *Religion in Britain since 1945: Believing without Belonging* (Oxford: Blackwell, 1994).

Davie, Grace, Paul Heelas and Linda Woodhead, eds. *Predicting Religion* (Aldershot: Ashgate, 2003).

Frost, Michael. *The Road to Missional* (Grand Rapids: Baker, 2011).

Furlong, Monica. *C of E: The State It's In* (London: Hodder & Stoughton, 2000).

Gibbs, Eddie. *The Rebirth of the Church* (Grand Rapids: Baker, 2013).

Goodhew, David, ed. *Church Growth in Britain 1980 to the Present* (Farnham: Ashgate, 2012).

Richard Edwin Koenig. *A Creative Minority: The Church in a New Age* (Minneapolis: Augsburg, 1971).

Kreider, Alan, Eleanor Kreider and Paulus Widjaja. *A Culture of Peace: God's Vision for the Church* (Intercourse, PA: Good Books, 2005).

McDowell, Peter. *At Home in Exile* (Belfast: Contemporary Christianity, 2012).

Murray, Stuart. *Church after Christendom* (Milton Keynes: Paternoster, 2004).

Murray, Stuart. *Post-Christendom* (Carlisle: Paternoster, 2004).

Peppiatt, Lucy. *The Disciple* (Eugene, OR: Cascade, 2012).

Roth, John, ed. *Constantine Revisited* (Eugene, OR: Pickwick, 2013).

Roxburgh, Alan. *The Missionary Congregation, Leadership, and Liminality* (New York: Continuum, 1997).

Smith, C. Christopher and John Pattison. *Slow Church: Cultivating Community in the Patient Way of Jesus* (Downers Grove: IVP, 2014).

Standing, Roger. *As a Fire by Burning* (London: SCM Press, 2013).

Tennent, Timothy. *Theology in the Context of World Christianity* (Grand Rapids: Zondervan, 2007).

Wright, Christopher. *The Mission of God: Unlocking the Bible's Grand Narrative* (Downers Grove: IVP, 2006).

Wright, Nigel. *New Baptists, New Agenda* (Carlisle: Paternoster, 2002).

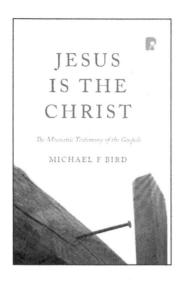

JESUS
IS THE
CHRIST

The Messianic Testimony of the Gospels

MICHAEL F BIRD

Jesus is the Christ

The Messianic Testimony of the Gospels

Michael F. Bird

In this book Michael Bird engages the subject of the messianism of the four Gospels. While the title and role of 'Messiah' ascribed to Jesus in the Gospels has long been regarded as a late add on, a fabricate claim, or an insignificant feature, Bird argues in contrast that the messianic claims are the most significant for the portrayal of Jesus. Bird proceeds to show how the claim that 'Jesus is the Messiah' drives the purpose and shape of the Gospels. He describes how each Evangelist portrays Jesus as the Messiah of Israel and what they think was at stake in that claim.

Michael Bird tackles one of the hottest topics currently debated among New Testament scholars – what early believers understood by their confession that Jesus was the Christ, the promised Messiah of Israel. This is a splendid study, written by an expert in the field, in engaging style and displaying clarity of thought. There is much to be learnt on every page – **Paul Foster, lecturer in New Testament, Edinburgh University.**

978-1-84227-446-1

Light on Prophecy

Retrieving Word and Prophecy in Today's Church

Jennifer Campbell

The author correlates the vision and thinking of two powerful prophetic leaders: Hildegard of Bingen, a twelfth-century enclosed nun/mystic, and Dietrich Bonhoeffer, the twentieth-century German pastor/theologian executed by the Nazis. With a view to recovering a balanced and rounded theology of prophecy for the church today, she discusses the closely related workings of both the Word of God (viewed as Christ and the Scriptures) and the Holy Spirit in the works and lives of these famous Christians.

'Rarely do we encounter maturity, depth and wisdom when the subject at hand is the prophetic gift. Jenny Campbell's book is the exception. With rare insight she offers us a workable and thorough theology of Prophecy' – **Mike Breen, 3DM Global Leader.**

Jennifer Campbell is a lecturer in Christian Doctrine at Westminster Theological Centre, Cheltenham, UK. She is also the leader of Eaglesinflight.

978-1-84227-768-3

Multi-Voiced Church

Stuart & Sian Murray Williams

Multi-Voiced Church argues strongly and persuasively for churches in which everyone is important for the well-being and growth of the community. A multi-voiced church is necessary for genuine mission in today's complex world.

'Those who take the book to heart may find they have a share in making a significant contribution to helping local churches enjoy significant and lasting renewal.' – **Stephen Finamore, Principal of Bristol Baptist College.**

'*Multi-Voiced Church* is an important book that addresses the centuries-old abuse that stifles congregations and exhausts clergy – the silencing of the laity. It is bold, original and practical. Together they have written a multi-voiced book on multi-voiced church life. The medium and the message work together. Wonderful.' – **Alan and Eleanor Kreider, Associated Mennonite Biblical Seminary, Elkhart, Indiana (retired); authors** of *Worship and Mission After Christendom* **(2009)**

978-1-84227-766-9

Primitive Piety

A Journey from Suburban Mediocrity to Passionate Christianity

Ian Stackhouse

In *Primitive Piety* Ian Stackhouse takes us on a journey away from the safety and pleasantries of suburban piety and into a faith that is able to embrace the messiness as well as the paradoxes of the Christian faith.

In a culture in which there is every danger that we all look the same and speak the same, Stackhouse argues for a more gritty kind of faith – one that celebrates the oddity of the gospel, the eccentricity of the saints, and the utter uniqueness of each and every church.

Ian Stackhouse is the Pastoral Leader of Millmead, Guildford Baptist Church.

978-1-84227-786-7

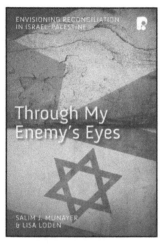

Through My Enemy's Eyes

Envisioning Reconciliation in Israel–Palestine

Salim Munayer and Lisa Loden

This unique book addresses reconciliation in the context of the Israeli Messianic Jewish and Palestinian Christian divide. This remarkable work, written in collaboration by a local Palestinian Christian and an Israeli Messianic Jew addresses head-on divisive theological issues (and their political implications); land, covenant, prophecy, eschatology. The struggle for reconciliation is painful and often extremely difficult for all of us. This work seeks to show a way forward.

'This is a unique conversation in which each partner gives full expression to all that they are and think and feel about themelves and the conflict in their land. Above all we come to share the hope and courage that shines through the pain and struggle.' *Christopher Wright, Langham Paternership.*

'Given the divides between their communities, this book is a remarkable achievement, a cry of hope from the land where Jesus walked.' *Chris Rice Duke Divinity School, US.*

Salim Munayer is on the faculty of Bethlehem Bible College, Bethlehem, Palestine and director of Musalaha Ministry of Reconciliation, Jerusalem, Israel. Lisa Loden is on the faculty of Nazareth Evangelical Theological Seminary, Nazareth, Israel, and Director of Advancing Professional Excellence, Israel.

978-1-84227-748-5 (e-book 978-1-84227-859-8)

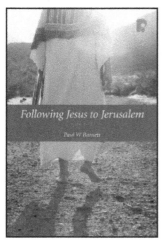

Following Jesus to Jerusalem

Luke 9–19

Paul Barnett

Taking the metaphor of life as a journey, Paul Barnett follows the journey of Jesus to Jerusalem and suggests that we journey with him. Barnett stresses the important place of kingdom in this and the ethics of Christian living which naturally follow from being in the presence of a humble saviour. More than a commentary, then, this important book challenges the way we live in the light of Jesus' last days and self-sacrifice. Paul Barnett expounds Luke, chapters 9–19, with the intention of provoking faith and faithulness in the lives of Jesus' followers today.

Paul Barnett is the former Bishop of North Sydney and lecturer in New Testament, Moore College, Syndey, Ausralia.

978-1-84227-767-6 (e-book 978-1-84227-859-8)